THE
TAROT
COLORING BOOK

BY
THERESA REED

sounds true
BOULDER, COLORADO

Sounds True
Boulder, CO 80306

Published 2016

Cover and book design by Lisa Kerans
Card illustrations by Pamela Colman Smith, 1910
Background Patterns © Shutterstock

Printed in Korea

Library of Congress Cataloging-in-Publication Data
Names: Reed, Theresa (Tarot Reader), author.
Title: The Tarot coloring book / by Theresa Reed.
Description: Boulder, CO : Sounds True, 2016.
Identifiers: LCCN 2016011043 | ISBN 9781622037902
Subjects: LCSH: Tarot.
Classification: LCC BF1879.T2 R44 2016 | DDC 133.3/2424—dc23
LC record available at http://lccn.loc.gov/2016011043

10 9 8 7 6 5 4 3 2 1

DEDICATION

For Terry, Megan, and Nick.

CONTENTS

FOREWORD

When I first encountered the Rider Waite Tarot nearly half a century ago, I immediately fell in love with the brightly colored pictorial scenes. I yearned for the ability to discover things about myself and others by manipulating these pieces of cardboard. Yet when I tried to learn their meanings, I nearly gave up in despair because the books told me I had to memorize all the meanings of the cards first. I stared at lists until my eyes (and brain) clouded over, but I could never recall what they said when faced with a layout. Luckily, courses in theatrical improvisation and literary symbolism saved the day as I learned to improvise metaphorically relevant tales based on the pictures.

What I longed for was a hands-on, playful approach to learning the cards, something where all my senses could be employed, where I could learn by doing. I've written books explaining methods that helped me, but they are still text-heavy and some people never get past the print.

Here's a book that goes beyond what I imagined. To call it just a coloring book is missing the point. Rather, it can be a total immersion experience in the Tarot. The text for each card is just enough to stimulate your imagination and evoke personal associations while you see the pictures come alive beneath your hands.

The smell and feel of crayons (I prefer them) puts you in an open, childlike state that encourages experimentation—like the first card, the Fool. Moving your hands as you color has you moving energy like the Magician, an empowering act of will. Take a moment to center yourself, as Theresa suggests, to access the sixth-sense, intuitive center of the High Priestess. Taste the fruits of the earth with the Empress (grains, fruit, or chocolate are highly recommended!), and you'll never forget her gifts. See how the Emperor helps you establish a firm foundation for your Tarot practice. Read the text out loud to hear the Hierophant's teachings. Employing all your senses ensures that a multidimensional Tarot comes to life at every level of your body. It's a deep knowing you'll never forget.

You are so lucky to have Theresa Reed as your guide and companion in getting to know the cards. She combines a modern, no-nonsense, street-savvy approach to Tarot with a generous and soulful heart. Plus, Theresa is practically experienced in professionally helping thousands face life's problems and mysteries. This is a woman who focuses on real issues and passes her wisdom on to you. Follow along with her example spreads by laying out the cards from your own deck to see what I mean. Theresa's succinct and sassy advice—from getting started to going professional—says it all.

MARY K. GREER
author of *21 Ways to Read a Tarot Card*
October 22, 2015

INTRODUCTION

Not everyone knows this about me, but in addition to being a Tarot reader (my main gig), I also teach yoga and run a small, quirky yoga studio. Tarot and yoga are like my kids—I couldn't possibly choose a "favorite." Both inspire and sometimes challenge me, and both bring beautiful qualities into my life.

But things weren't always so peachy keen. Back when I began my yoga-teacher-training program more than a decade ago, I had no problem understanding yogic philosophy. Easy peasy. Yamas and niyamas? No problema. I was down with the spiritual side of yoga, but I really struggled to master the kinesthetic and anatomical aspects of teaching yoga.

Honestly, when it came to memorizing parts of the human anatomy, I felt like the classroom dunce.

I am not a scientific person in any way, shape, or form. And, oh, those long names! *Meniscus. Iliopsoas. Piriformis.* How on earth was I ever going to remember which was which body part . . . or how to pronounce those long science-y words? To say that I was intimidated is an understatement. I was terrified that I would never "get it."

Fortunately, I managed to get my hands on a copy of the classic *Anatomy Coloring Book*, which allowed me to learn human anatomy in a fun and easy way. This book totally rocked my world. I no longer felt afraid and overwhelmed. In fact, I aced my exam and was the top student in my class for the anatomy portion! (Dunce no longer!)

This experience reminded me that different people learn in different ways. Some peeps are visual learners, others need audio, others need tons of repetition or face-to-face instruction as opposed to an online or virtual classroom.

Me? I tend to learn things best when I am learning *experientially*. I need to get hands-on—dig in, touch things, scribble, color, make notes in the margins, and really have an immersive experience with whatever I'm trying to understand—and that's how lessons sink in for me. That's just how I

am wired—and I know I'm not alone in this regard. (Maybe you're wired like this, too.)

So when the nice folks at Sounds True approached me and asked if I'd like to create a coloring book to help total beginners learn how to do Tarot, I could not say "Yes!" fast enough.

Tarot, much like anatomy, requires a certain degree of memorization. You've got to remember what the cards mean, what certain symbols represent, what certain colors signify, and what it means when certain cards show up side by side, upside down, or in other configurations. All of this becomes easier and more instinctual over time, but initially, when you're a Tarot newbie? It's a lot to hold in your brain.

That's why I was so thrilled to be invited to create this coloring book—a fun, simple introduction to Tarot where you can color your way through the deck, one card at a time, grasping the basics as you go along.

Over the years, I've taught Tarot to many curious seekers. Just like me back in that anatomy class, most Tarot newbies feel that the deck is so complicated, and they worry they'll never "get it." How I wish there would have been a coloring book for Tarot back in ye olden days! But now I don't have to wish—and neither do you. It's here, and you're holding it in your hands.

As you color the images, you'll find yourself seeing symbols that you may not have noticed before. You'll see stories and patterns begin to emerge. You'll find your own meanings while learning the traditional ones. The deck will become more familiar to you—like a good friend who wants to help you, not a stranger spouting confusing nonsense.

Tarot doesn't have to be so intimidating—and by the time you reach the end of this coloring book, you'll be well on your way to becoming a confident Tarot reader. I'm so excited for you.

So without further ado . . . grab your coloring gear, and let's start talkin' Tarot!

HOW TO USE
THIS COLORING BOOK

There are many ways to use this coloring book. Feel free to do what feels right to you, but here is what I suggest.

STEP 1 Get a Tarot Deck

I recommend that you purchase the Rider Waite Tarot Deck, which is considered the "classic" or "gold standard" of Tarot decks—a must-own deck for any Tarot lover.

The images in this coloring book are modeled off the images in the original guide to the Rider Waite Tarot, *The Pictorial Key to the Tarot,* by A. E. Waite, so as you color the images in this book, you can pull out the corresponding Rider Waite card and keep it beside you as a "model" or "coloring guide."

You can purchase the Rider Waite Tarot Deck at online retailers that sell books or at your friendly local metaphysical shop. Just march in and say to the clerk, "I'd like a Rider Waite Tarot Deck, please and thank you." They'll know what you're talking about.

STEP 2 Gather Your Coloring Supplies

Got your deck? Great. Now get a set of crayons or colored pencils that you like. Felt tip pens can work, but they may bleed through the paper, so I don't recommend them. If you want to get supercrafty, get some glitter, stickers, washi tape, or gems to add some personal flair!

STEP 3 Choose a Peaceful Time

When you're ready for a coloring session, pick a quiet time when you won't be disturbed. First thing in the morning may work for some, while others might find this practice to be more relaxing at the end of the day. Coloring is a meditative act, so a peaceful environment is best.

STEP 4 Set the Scene

Organize your workspace so that you feel centered and peaceful. If you like, you may wish to light a candle or a stick of incense. Soft music in the background can create a lovely ambience.

STEP 5 Begin Coloring!

You'll notice that each coloring page in this book includes some helpful info about the card you're about to color—like what this card usually means when it pops up in a reading and so on. I recommend reading this info before you start coloring. If you'd like, take a moment to close your eyes and soak in the information. Then, color away!

MOST OF ALL Do It Your Way

There's no "correct" way to color each card. This is your coloring book and your journey!

You may want to start with the background and work your way to the center of the card. Or you may be called to start on one symbol that is catching your eye. You might want to glance at the corresponding card from the Rider Waite deck and color the card in your book exactly the same way, creating a mirror image. Or you might want to go wild, defy traditions, and do a totally different color scheme. Go ahead!

As I mentioned above, coloring is a meditative act. As you continue working on the image, you may find yourself becoming more relaxed. The more you lean in to this feeling, the more you may discover in the Tarot.

REFLECT AND MOVE ALONG

When you are done coloring each card, take a moment to examine the finished image.

What did you learn about the card? What do you feel is the essence of it? It's great to understand the general meaning of each card. But when you are doing a Tarot reading, try to forget what "the pros" think and trust your personal instincts. Take your time and notice any thoughts that arise as you color along. Do certain cards trigger strong emotions for you? Do certain cards remind you of someone you know or a situation that's currently going on in your life? Is the card delivering a particular message to you right now? Is there a lesson or story that you suddenly recall?

Gaze at the illustration for a few moments and then jot down any thoughts, interpretations, or feelings that emerge in the space following the description of each card or in a journal.

Enjoy your handiwork, and then move on as you feel called.

Most of all, try not to become discouraged if you forget what certain cards are called or what they signify or if you get confused as you move along. Learning how to do Tarot is just like any other skill (like bike riding, playing the piano, making sushi, or becoming a superfly rapper). The more you practice, the more intuitive and instinctual the process will become. Keep practicing!

A QUICK INTRO TO TAROT

"When should I start my own business?"
"Should I try to negotiate a better offer . . .
or back off?"
"What do I need to know about this hot new guy
I just met?"
"Why do I have such a weird feeling about this
potential job opportunity?"

Got questions? Tarot's got answers.

Tarot is a practical—and mystical—tool for intuitive reasoning and decision making.

Learning how to read a Tarot deck can help you weigh options, identify unseen opportunities, avoid pitfalls, and confirm that your "hunches" are correct. I believe that everyone—yes, everyone—is born with intuitive abilities. We all get "funny feelings" and "flashes of insight" and "solutions" that seem to pop out of nowhere. The more you use your Tarot deck, the more you'll connect to your intuition, and the stronger your abilities will become.

Plus: it's fun!

Before we dive into the coloring portion of this book, the following chapters provide some info about what Tarot is and isn't, where it came from, and how you can use Tarot to answer questions and solve problems in your everyday life.

A (BRIEF) HISTORY OF TAROT AND THE ORIGIN OF THE RIDER WAITE DECK

Where did Tarot begin?
Who started it?
And why?

Confession: I am not a Tarot history scholar. Some people love to geek out over the history of Tarot, but that's never been my jam. (I'd rather eat a delicious, buttery croissant rather than learn the entire history of French baking, you know?)

But here's a zippy, condensed version of the history of Tarot, just to give you the basics:

- Tarot started in Italy during the 1400s. Back then, the early decks were called *carte da trionfi,* or "triumph cards." It does appear that the first Tarot decks were created as a game (they are still played as a game in many parts of the world to this day).

- Tarot cards were rare and expensive—a privilege of the upper classes—until the invention of mass printing in the mid-1400s.

- By the 1500s, more people were able to get their mitts on a deck of Tarot cards, and their popularity began to grow.

- In the late 1700s, a guy named Jean-Baptiste Alliette, often known as "Etteilla," published one of the world's first books on Tarot. In the book, he described how these cards could be used to understand conflicts, make wise decisions, and even predict likely future events. This book created a bump in Tarot popularity. (And triggered a few raised eyebrows and objections from certain religious leaders who were not feelin' it.)

- In the 1900s, Tarot experienced another surge in popularity when a guy named Arthur

Edward Waite commissioned artist Pamela Colman Smith to create a new Tarot deck: the Rider Waite deck. Even today, this deck is considered the "gold standard" of Tarot decks, a timeless classic.

- Today? Tarot continues to come "out of the shadows" and is finally being celebrated and accepted for what it is: a tool for awareness, divination, and conscious decision making!

Lots of celebrities have openly expressed their Tarot love. Some reportedly have a Tarot card reader in their business entourage. (Um, Hollywood celebs, call me if a spot ever opens up. I am in!).

Tarot is beginning to enter "the mainstream," and lots of artists are producing whimsical, unconventional Tarot decks—everything from vampire-themed Tarot decks to decks featuring cats wearing Victorian costumes (a favorite of mine!). More and more people are recognizing that Tarot is a fun, useful tool—there's nothing inherently "spooky" about it.

That brings us up to date, historically speaking. If you're a passionate history buff and you want to dive deep into the history of Tarot, I recommend reading *The Tarot: History, Symbolism, and Divination* by Robert Place—an excellent and very thorough book on this topic.

Now that our mini-history lesson is complete, let's move on to discuss colors!

ALL THOSE COLORS IN THE DECK: WHAT DO THEY MEAN?

In the world of Tarot, every color holds meaning and significance.

When an artist is creating a new Tarot deck, she's not choosing colors randomly—she's choosing each color with thoughtfulness and intention.

This is certainly true for the Rider Waite deck.

The colors you see on the cards in the Rider Waite deck are not accidental. Each one represents a specific quality or emotion.

Here is a general guide to the colors that show up in the Rider Waite deck:

BLACK negativity, evil, transformation

BLUE peace, spirituality, aspiration, tranquility

BROWN earth, ground, stability, commitment

GRAY depression, mystery

GREEN nature, renewal, vitality, prosperity, abundance

ORANGE success, aspiration, fun

PURPLE spirituality, ideals, wisdom, royalty, psychic

RED vitality, love, passion, action, danger

SILVER illumination, clarity, awareness

WHITE purity, peace, innocence

YELLOW intelligence, creativity, student, positivity, healing

On the description of each card, I list the traditional colors in the Rider Waite deck for quick reference. Feel free to take a peek at your deck as you color. But remember, you've got options.

You can color the images in this book so that each matches the corresponding card in the Rider Waite deck exactly, if that is your preference. Or you can break away from convention and color the cards your own way, using nontraditional colors. It's up to you. Whatever feels most enjoyable, relaxing, and fun is the way to go!

WHAT DOES "DOING TAROT" OR "READING TAROT" ACTUALLY MEAN?

When you "read Tarot" or "do Tarot" (same thing) this is what's happening:

- You come up with a question. (Or if you are doing a reading for someone else, such as a friend, family member, or client, you ask them to come up with a question.)
- You sit with that question for a moment, taking a deep breath or two, letting it sink in.
- You shuffle and cut your deck of Tarot cards.
- Then you pull out a single card (or, if you're being fancy, you pull out several cards to create a "spread").
- You gaze at the card (or cards) and see what is revealed to you. (You might refer to the reference book that came with your deck if you're drawing a total blank, or your "gut" might give you a strong message or interpretation—no book consultation required.)

That's pretty much it: come up with a question, shuffle, cut, pull out a card, stare at it, blammo—epiphany. Maybe I'm exaggerating on the epiphany part. For you, it may be a gentle knowing or a little intuitive nudge. That's Tarot in a nutshell.

Okay, perhaps I'm being a little overly simplistic, but, honestly, not by much! Anybody can learn how to do Tarot. The process is simple—the tricky part is getting completely calm, centered, and focused so that when you pull out a card and gaze at it, your intuition can actually "speak" to you instead of getting drowned out by all the chatter and stresses and monkey-mind stuff that typically crowd your brain.

Sometimes a card will show up upside down when you place it for a reading. In the Tarot world, this is called a *reversal*. Some Tarot readers take the reversal into account, while others treat the card as if it's right side up and don't "read into" the reversal. Either way, you can deliver a powerful reading. But I recommend giving reversals a whirl, because reversals can add subtle nuances to your readings, and, personally, I love that!

TEN WAYS TO USE TAROT IN YOUR EVERYDAY LIFE

Tarot can be used in a lot of different areas of your life. You can use it for the following:

- General decision making ("This or that?" "Rent or buy?" "Taco or burger?")
- Understanding the best way to help a loved one ("How can I support Mom right now?")
- Coming up with creative ideas ("What should I blog about this week?")
- Finding strategies for sticky situations ("What's the best way to proceed with ___?")
- Mapping out plans for the future ("What should I focus on next year?")
- Seeing the potential in a situation ("I feel stuck. What's the silver lining for ___?")
- A conversation prompt ("How does this card make you feel?")
- Avoiding pitfalls by looking at potential roadblocks and outcomes ("What is one challenge that's likely to come up if I choose ___?")
- Timing ("Now or later?" "Move forward or back off for now?")
- Entertaining your friends! ("Anybody got a question?")

If you want to learn more about how to do Tarot for yourself or your friends—including simple one-, two-, and three-card spreads that are great for beginners—check out chapter 11, "Spreads and Layouts."

If you're ready to get acquainted with each card in the deck—and start coloring!—then just turn the page.

THE MAJOR ARCANA

Every Tarot deck has two types of cards: Major
Arcana and Minor Arcana. There are twenty-two
Major Arcana cards and fifty-six Minor Arcana cards
for a total of seventy-eight cards per Tarot deck.

We're going to begin our Tarot coloring journey
with the Major Arcana.

Major Arcana cards represent the bigger spiritual picture: the big, deep, powerful forces that may
be creating opportunities or obstacles to our personal growth. Major Arcana cards are sometimes
called "trumps" or "trump cards," but in this coloring
book, we're going to stick with "Major Arcana."

THE FOOL

Card Number: 0

In our modern culture, calling someone a "fool" means you think they are reckless or stupid. But in the Tarot world, the Fool is no dummy.

The Fool represents someone embarking on a new adventure. Brave. Curious. Playful. The Fool is willing to put it all out there and try something new. If you've ever loaded up your car for a spontaneous road trip, ready to embrace whatever lies ahead, you have felt the thrilling, adventurous energy of the Fool. The Fool card is number 0, which represents nothingness, unlimited potential, or what Zen Buddhism calls "the beginner's mind." This card represents new beginnings, risks, and a leap of faith.

REVERSED (UPSIDE DOWN)

The Fool becomes hesitant. He pulls back from the edge. Is this wisdom or doubt? Are you staying in your comfort zone out of fear? Or are you simply not ready to move forward? If this card comes up for you in a reading, you might want to examine how fear may be playing a role in your life. The Fool reversed can also represent recklessness, immaturity, and impulse, not looking before leaping.

NOTICE THE SYMBOLS

A CLIFF The Fool is standing awfully close to the edge of the cliff—yikes!—yet he seems confident and joyful. The Fool craves adventure, even a bit of danger, but he knows his limits.

THE DOG The Fool has a small dog as a companion. The dog leaps playfully, perhaps mimicking his master's jubilant energy. The journey might be short or long, but the Fool won't be traveling alone.

A ROSE In the Tarot world, roses often symbolize freedom—particularly sensual or sexual freedom. The Fool might enjoy some, ahem, liberated "pleasures" in the near future.

BOOTS Those boots were made for walking! The Fool is geared up and ready for the journey ahead.

COLORS In the Rider Waite deck, the Fool is wearing a green, black, and yellow tunic over a white shirt with yellow boots. His rose and dog are both white. The sky is yellow with a white sun. The jagged mountains on the horizon are blue and white. (Peek at your deck to check out the color scheme in more detail.)

How do you want to color in The Fool? Which colors make you feel like taking a big, brave step? Go for it!

THE FOOL .

THE MAGICIAN

Card Number: 1

The Magician symbolizes the ability to direct your energy toward the things you wish to accomplish.

Unlike the carefree Fool, the Magician is ready to get down to business. His tools are laid out before him, and his stance is powerful. With a wand pointed to the heavens and a finger to the earth, this crafty trickster sets his intention and focuses his will on manifesting a goal.

Think about the times that you've wanted something so badly, you mustered every ounce of your power to make that happen. The Magician represents that level of willpower. This card also means skill, talent, and having all the tools you need to make epic stuff happen. The power is yours. It's up to you to stand in that power. So mote it be, indeed.

REVERSED

The Magician lacks the skills and gumption needed to succeed. This could be due to weakness, laziness, or incompetence. The power becomes blocked, and, in some cases, there may be a tendency to blame others for your inability to manifest your goals. The reversed Magician isn't just negative thinking—it can also symbolize an abuse of power. How are you taking responsibility for where you are . . . or aren't? Empowerment begins within.

NOTICE THE SYMBOLS

THE INFINITY SYMBOL ABOVE HIS HEAD Also called a "lemniscate," this represents the endless energy in the universe. Energy is neither good nor bad; it's just available for our use. It's up to you to set the right intention and then take action.

THE SNAKE BELT AROUND HIS WAIST Snakes symbolize renewal and rebirth. What are you ready to transform?

A WAND, CUP, PENTACLES, AND SWORD ON THE TABLE Like a chef's *mise en place,* these are his tools and represent the four elements: fire, water, earth, and air. The Magician has all the resources he needs to succeed. He brings his talent and willpower to the table and bam—magic happens!

COLORS In the Rider Waite deck, the Magician wears a bright red robe over a white gown. His table is a reddish orange. The cup and pentacles are yellow, while the sword is silver. He has two wands—a brown one on the table and a white one in his left hand. The flowers around him are red roses and white lilies.

Which colors make you feel powerful?

THE MAGICIAN.

THE HIGH PRIESTESS

Card Number: 2

The High Priestess represents the mystical side of life and intuitive abilities.

The first female in the deck, the High Priestess moves in mysterious ways. She's got secrets, and she's not sharing them. The only way to find the truth is by going within. It's all about inner power. Unlike the active yang energy of the Magician, the High Priestess is yin—introspective and receptive. She doesn't have to chase the answers—they just come to her. She doesn't force things—she simply "knows." This is the time to trust your gut. Keep your mouth shut and your third eye open.

REVERSED

When the High Priestess shows up reversed in a Tarot reading, she becomes more active and involved with the outer world, and this may cause her to lose sight of her inner guidance. If you've ever ignored the quiet voice within—and later regretted it—that's what this reversal is talkin' about.

NOTICE THE SYMBOLS

THE PILLARS The pillars represent the entrance of Solomon's Temple. Marked with a *B* for *Boaz* and a *J* for *Jachin* (the names of the two pillars in the temple in Jerusalem), they represent duality and balance.

THE MOON BENEATH HER FEET The moon represents intuition, change, and things that are hidden in the dark.

THE CURTAIN What's on the other side of that curtain? The curtain represents the doorway to our subconscious.

THE POMEGRANATE A pomegranate is filled with seeds, a symbol of fertility.

THE SCROLL Secret, secret, she's got a secret! The scroll symbolizes hidden knowledge. What's on that scroll? That's for her to know and you to find out.

COLORS In the Rider Waite deck, the High Priestess wears a robe of sky blue and white and a white crown on her head. The moon beneath her foot is bright yellow. The curtain is adorned with yellow-and-red pomegranates. The pillars are black and white.

Which colors make you feel connected to your inner wisdom?

THE HIGH PRIESTESS

THE EMPRESS

Card Number: 3

*The Empress represents savoring the fruits of your labor,
relishing the rewards that you have rightfully earned.*

In Tarot, the Empress is the queen bee and Mother Earth all rolled up into one. She's passionate but also motherly. Sexy. Nurturing. Her theme song is "I Am Woman" with its opening line, "I am woman, hear me roar." Unlike the mysterious, secretive High Priestess, the Empress is living life full-out and full-on. She lives for pleasure and sensuality, abundance, and fertility. Birth, marriage, and pregnancy (literal pregnancy or creative pregnancy, like "birthing" a new project or book) all fall under this luscious card.

REVERSED

The Empress loses her luster . . . and her lust for life. The energy is unproductive, and results are scant at best. Think barren soil, creative blocks, or the dissolution of a relationship. The urge to nurture becomes blocked or turned off entirely. (Remember the disturbing film *Mommie Dearest*? That's an extreme representation of the Empress reversed!)

This reversal can also represent the "mother martyr" who takes care of everyone else's needs except her own. How are you caring for yourself? Remember: always put your own oxygen mask on first before assisting others.

NOTICE THE SYMBOLS

THE WATERFALL The flowing water behind the Empress symbolizes the life force that is always flowing within us and around us.

THE CROWN OF STARS The twelve stars are the twelve signs of the zodiac. She's tapping into universal energy. Big power.

THE WHEAT The chaffs of wheat are the fruits of her labor. Think harvest. You reap what you sow, and she's got a whole field at her feet.

A HEART-SHAPED SHIELD WITH THE VENUS SYMBOL Protection and love. This is as motherly as it gets.

THE SCEPTER She's large and in charge, and this scepter reminds you of her dominion.

COLORS In the Rider Waite deck, the Empress kicks back on a red throne. She's wearing a white robe with red flowers. Her hair is yellow. The waterfall is clear blue, and the wheat is yellow, as is the sky. Green trees dot the background.

Which colors make you feel abundant?

III

THE EMPRESS.

THE EMPEROR

Card Number: 4

The Emperor represents hard work, discipline, and the structures that create security.

The Empress contains the laws of nature—but the Emperor is the law of society. This serious-looking fellow is all about authority and power. There is no time for spontaneity and frivolity when he shows up in a Tarot reading—he wants structure, order, and control.

While that may sound boring, this is the card you want to see if you are looking to get things organized or if you want more stability. He's the ultimate father figure, always willing and able to provide. You may not like his rules, but he's always got your back.

REVERSED

When you turn the Emperor upside down, he loses his grip on power or becomes power hungry. The empire crumbles, for there is nothing stable to sustain it. The energy becomes harsh or weak—sometimes both, because often when we are hurt, we tend to lash out and hurt others. The Emperor reversed can signify problems with authority or daddy issues. It can also represent a lack of security or a lack of the willingness and maturity needed to create it.

NOTICE THE SYMBOLS

THRONE WITH RAMS' HEADS Connected with the astrological sign of Aries, the ram is a symbol of leadership, and this throne says he's the boss.

ARMOR If you peek under his robe, you'll see he's wearing a suit of armor. This tells you that he's protected and not much can get to him.

THE MOUNTAINS The mountains represent the hard work he's endured to get where he's at. The Emperor has earned that crown through his determination and strength.

THE ANKH The ankh is a symbol of life and death. I told you this guy means serious business!

COLORS In the Rider Waite deck, the Emperor wears a red robe, symbolic of his power. His crown and staff are gold. His throne is stone gray, and his armor is silver. The mountains and background are light brown. There is a small blue river flowing in the background.

Which colors make you feel powerful, orderly, or stable?

IV

THE EMPEROR.

THE HIEROPHANT

Card Number: 5

The Hierophant represents spiritual teachings and dogma.
He's concerned with upholding the traditions that give meaning to our lives.

Like the Emperor, the Hierophant is concerned with rules and order. Decked out in regal clothing like a pope, the Hierophant can symbolize religious rites such as weddings or a wise teacher, counselor, or mentor who guides his students toward higher learning. Conformity, respect for authority, and orthodox approaches all fall under the Hierophant's reign. Follow the path well trod by the wise elders who have gone before you. The rules are in place for a reason.

REVERSED

When we reverse the Hierophant, it's kind of like throwing the rules out the window. Time to examine your beliefs. Are they valid, or are you just blindly following someone else's rulebook? A reversed Hierophant indicates nonconformity, originality, and a willingness to take risks. Rebellion, anarchy, and an overthrow of the old ways. A new world order. Fighting "the man." Seeing a reversed Hierophant and getting a "bad vibe"? This reversal can also symbolize an abuse of power or an authority figure who takes advantage of his or her position.

NOTICE THE SYMBOLS

POPE REGALIA His religious gear indicates that he's a religious authority, a bridge between heaven and earth.

THE HAND This gesture symbolizes a benediction. He's giving his blessing.

THE KEYS These represent spiritual knowledge. He's got the keys to the kingdom! That's why those two guys are kneeling before him—they are seekers of spiritual wisdom.

COLORS In the Rider Waite deck, the Hierophant wears a red robe with white trim and sleeves. His headdress and staff are golden yellow. His throne is gray, and the platform underneath his feet is red. The keys are yellow. The followers at his feet wear floral robes with yellow trim. One has a robe with red roses, and the other a blue robe with white lilies.

Which colors spring to mind when you think about a wise teacher or elder?

THE HIEROPHANT

THE LOVERS

Card Number: 6

The Lovers symbolizes a relationship that is loving and trusting.

When asking about matters of the heart, the Lovers is the card you want to see in a Tarot reading. After all, it's pretty straightforward with the depiction of the naked couple! Ooh la la! Mutual attraction and compatibility. Marriage or commitment. Two people coming together in a happy, healthy way. This isn't always romantic in nature—the partnership could also be a business connection or friendship. This card can also represent temptation or a big choice. If you are faced with a major decision, trust your higher guidance to find the right path. Lean in to the choice that feels most like "love."

REVERSED

When reversed, the Lovers indicates dysfunction. A relationship turns sour or destructive. Someone wants out. A commitment-phobe or philanderer. What took a lifetime to build is destroyed through mistrust or an indiscretion. The Lovers reversed can also symbolize an unwillingness to compromise or communicate. Is your star employee thinking about making a sudden exit? Are you feeling iffy about your new lover, with one foot halfway out the door? The Lovers reversed invites you to ask, "What's up with that?"

NOTICE THE SYMBOLS

THE SNAKE The image of the serpent represents temptation. Forbidden fruit. Wanna bite that apple?

THE TREES Speaking of apple, there is an apple tree behind the female, believed to be the Tree of Knowledge of Good and Evil. The one behind the male is the Tree of Life. Welcome to the Garden of Eden.

THE ANGEL This is the Archangel Raphael, who is often associated with healing. Love cures all.

THE NAKED COUPLE Nudity is a symbol of vulnerability and expressing oneself honestly. Whip off that fig leaf. No more hiding. It's time to share your truth!

COLORS In the Rider Waite deck, the naked couple is peach-colored. The angel has a purple robe, red wings, and a headdress of red and green. The sun is bright yellow, and the mountain is brown. The serpent and the ground are both green. The tree behind the woman has red fruits and green leaves, while the one behind the male has red and yellow flames.

Which colors make you feel romantic, loved, and adored?

THE LOVERS.

THE CHARIOT

Card Number: 7

The Chariot symbolizes being "in the driver's seat" and in control.

The figure in the Chariot has a wand in his hand and a determined look on his face. He's going places, and not much is going to get in his way. If he encounters an obstacle, he'll move right past it because he's got places to go and things to conquer (not to mention sweet wheels!). You've found the vehicle you need to progress on your journey. Full speed ahead! There is a conquest in the rearview mirror and a victory in sight. Triumph is yours!

REVERSED

The path becomes riddled with obstacles. The bigger problem? You've lost sight of your goals or have given up control. This is like running out of gas or allowing an incompetent navigator to sit in the driver's seat. Suddenly you're no longer on your right path and are headed for a crash. Find an alternate route or abandon course.

NOTICE THE SYMBOLS

THE SPHINXES In some Tarot decks, the Chariot is being pulled by horses, but in the Rider Waite, we see two sphinxes. These represent duality or opposing forces. The Charioteer has these forces under his control—without any reins. That's real power.

THE CHARIOT The vehicle that swiftly takes you forward. What are you driving? What drives you?

THE WAND The wand is a symbol of power and dominion. This guy's in control.

THE MOONS The moon represents the subconscious or hidden forces that motivate us. A secret agenda perhaps?

COLORS In the Rider Waite deck, one sphinx is black and the other is white. The background is yellow, and the curtains of the chariot are blue with white symbols. His chariot is gray with a small blue winged symbol and a red one below it. The moons are pale yellow, as is his crown. His armor is black and white. The buildings in the background are white with red roofs.

Which colors make you feel triumphant, driven, or focused on victory?

VII

THE CHARIOT.

STRENGTH

Card Number: 8 (in some decks, 11)

Strength symbolizes the inner power and courage to handle life's challenges.

Strength symbolizes the confidence that arises when we take responsibility for our own problems, taking matters into our own strong, capable hands.

Unlike the Chariot, the Strength card is in control, but there is no need for force. Instead, she gently tames the lion by taking his jaws in her hands. When have you found yourself in a situation where it was better to take a firm but sensitive approach? You were channeling the energy of this card. This is inner strength and the wisdom to do the right thing, even if it seems difficult. It's also a symbol of "taming inner demons."

REVERSED

Turn Strength upside down and we get weak in the knees. Cowardice. Insecurity. Instead of grappling with our issues, we look to someone else to take them off our hands. Can you remember a time when you threw in the towel in the face of a challenge? Think wimping out, the cowardly lion.

NOTICE THE SYMBOLS

INFINITY SYMBOL As with the Magician, we see the infinity symbol above her head—a sign of infinite energy available for her use. She's got the power!

THE LION The lion represents our animal instincts or ego. Taming the beast within. Roar!

THE GARLAND AND BELT OF ROSES These represent a triumph, a big win, or completion. Holding strong and moving toward victory.

COLORS In the Rider Waite deck, the background is yellow. The lion is orange. The woman is blonde and wearing a white robe. Her garland and belt have green leaves and red roses. The ground and trees are light green and the mountain is blue.

Which colors make you feel strong?

THE HERMIT

Card Number: 9

The Hermit indicates that it's time to pull back and to reflect. Quiet contemplation.

Have you ever felt as if you needed to be alone to sort out your feelings and hear yourself think? If so, you already have an idea of what the Hermit is about. He's not concerned with the external world. Instead he withdraws into himself with only a lantern to light the way. This is because the answers he seeks are not going to be found out there . . . they are inside.

The Hermit can also represent a spiritual guide or wise teacher. Maybe you're about to meet that teacher. Or maybe that teacher is you—you might just be playing that role for other people in your life.

REVERSED

The Hermit comes out of hiding and back into the world. This signifies a return—but it can also represent a return to the same ol' situation. Repeating your past mistakes. Not learning your lesson. Seeking answers in all the wrong places instead of turning within. The Hermit reversed can also indicate escapism or fear of other people. Think Howard Hughes.

NOTICE THE SYMBOLS

THE LANTERN The lantern lights the path, a symbol of a trusty guide that helps us find our way through the dark.

THE STAR If you peer into his lantern, you'll notice the six-pointed Star of David, which represents the light of God.

THE STAFF If you look closely, you'll see he's leaning on a staff. This is referred to as the "patriarchal staff"—a symbol of initiation and his authority as a teacher.

THE BEARD This is not a fashion statement! It's a symbol of wisdom and maturity.

COLORS In the Rider Waite deck, the background bluish gray. The Hermit's robe is gray, and his beard is white. He's standing on a white, snow-covered mountain. His staff is yellow, as is the light in the lantern.

Which colors make you feel a sense of introspection and solitude?

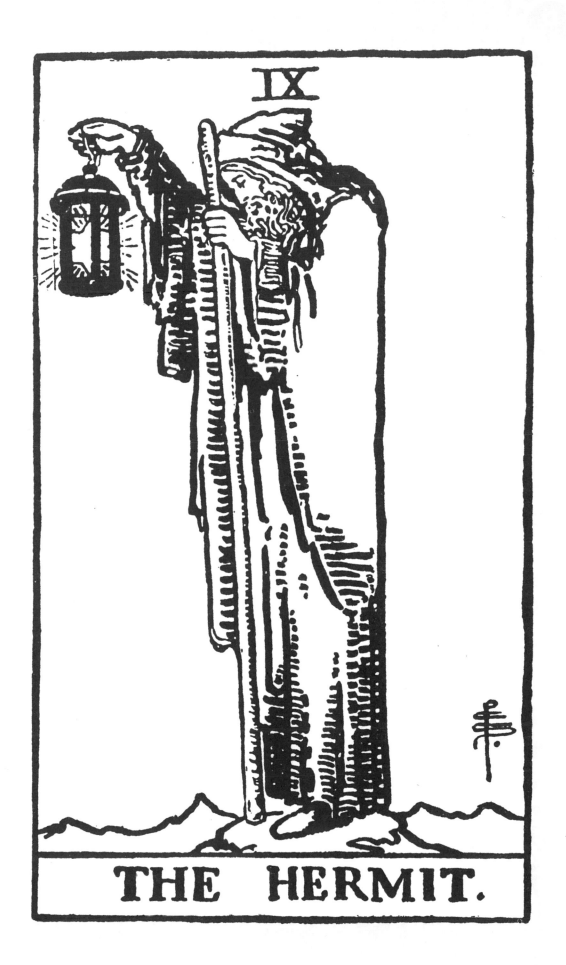

IX

THE HERMIT.

THE WHEEL OF FORTUNE

Card Number: 10

*Life moves in cycles, and the presence of the Wheel of Fortune
suggests an auspicious change is on the way.*

What goes down must come up! Whatever your circumstances are, change is afoot. A pivotal turn of events could set you on a different (usually better) course. This can be attributable to fate intervening on your behalf or the karmic consequences of past deeds coming due. Everyone gets their turn at the Wheel. Get ready for yours.

REVERSED

When you reverse the Wheel of Fortune, it indicates a reversal of fortune! A karmic cycle may be repeating itself all over again. Or you may be struggling to accept a change in circumstances. Another interpretation would be "limbo"—as in, everything is in flux and where it all ends up . . . no one knows. Do your best to roll with the uncertainty because sometimes that's all you can do. Karma's a bitch.

NOTICE THE SYMBOLS

THE WHEEL Big wheel keep on turning! Wheels signify cycles. Things are always changing, and nothing is permanent.

THE SPHINX The sphinx symbolizes fate or the mysteries of life. He is the guardian of the sacred.

THE SNAKE Snakes are a symbol of transformation. What are you ready to shed?

THE JACKAL-HEADED CREATURE This jackal-headed figure is Anubis, the guide to dead souls. He represents a new life cycle.

THE FOUR CREATURES READING BOOKS These figures represent the four elements: earth, fire, water, and air (or, in the Tarot world: Pentacles, Wands, Cups, and Swords). They can also symbolize the four seasons or the four fixed signs of the zodiac: Aquarius, Scorpio, Leo, and Taurus.

COLORS In the Rider Waite deck, the wheel is bright orange. The sphinx is blue, as is the sky. The winged creatures are yellow. The snake is orange, and Anubis is red. The clouds are white.

Which colors make you feel lucky or fortunate?

WHEEL of FORTUNE.

JUSTICE

Card Number: 11 (in some decks 8)

The Justice card is a reminder that we get what we deserve.

The consequences of past actions come due and things are fair, whether or not we think they are. This card can indicate legal matters. If you're dealing with the court system, it's likely that justice will prevail. It's also an indicator of choice. Weigh your options carefully. Aim for a fair decision. Seek balance. Justice demands truth, and this card can be a not-so-gentle nudge to remain completely honest in all your dealings.

REVERSED

Justice reversed is not the card you want to see if you're on trial—it portends an unfair outcome. Injustice or inequality. Justice delayed is justice denied. Unjust legal actions. It's also a sign of a karmic situation coming due, like payback for previous bad deeds. Justice reversed can indicate dishonesty or crooked behavior. Last, it's also a sign of poor decision making or a refusal to take responsibility for your choices. Bad judgment.

NOTICE THE SYMBOLS

THE SCALES Justice for all! These are a symbol of balance and equality.

THE SWORD Swords can symbolize ideas or the ability to cut through a situation to get to the heart of the matter. Truth is your weapon!

THE PILLARS The marble pillars represent duality and choices. Think of the karmic consequences before making a decision.

COLORS In the Rider Waite deck, the figure wears a bright red robe with green trim. His crown is yellow. The pillars are gray, and the curtain is violet. The sword is silver with a yellow handle, and the scales are yellow as well.

Which colors make you feel balanced, just, or fair?

THE HANGED MAN

Card Number: 12

The Hanged Man represents surrender, a period of waiting, a new perspective on a dilemma, and the ability to completely trust that everything will work out as it needs to.

The Hanged Man is hanging upside down, dangling by one foot in a seemingly precarious situation, yet he seems to be totally at peace. This is a guy who knows how to relax and let go. What does that boil down to? Faith. What are you ready and willing to release? What would improve in your life if you could just hang loose and let go? This card can also symbolize a worthy sacrifice.

REVERSED

When the Hanged Man is reversed, it can be interpreted as getting stuck or hung up. However, this is going to depend on the nature of the question you're asking and what you may be feeling. Some people interpret the Hanged Man reversed as "getting back on your feet," but it can also represent an inability to let go or understand someone else's point of view.

NOTICE THE SYMBOLS

THE HALO The halo indicates spirituality or enlightenment. Sometimes we need a new perspective to "see the light."

THE TREE Trees symbolize roots, learning, and new growth. In the Hanged Man, this tree is sometimes viewed as the World Tree from which Odin, the Norse god, hung in an effort to gain knowledge.

THE POSITION OF HIS LEGS He's not doing yoga, although this does indeed look like the "tree" position. The figure four represents the four directions of the earth: north, west, east, and south. It can also indicate a crossroads. Best way to choose a direction? Have faith in your gut instincts, and don't overthink it.

COLORS In the Rider Waite deck, the Hanged Man is wearing a blue tunic and red tights. His shoes are yellow. His hair is blond, and he has a halo of yellow around his head. The tree trunk is brown, and the leaves are green.
  Which colors make you feel calm?

THE HANGED MAN.

DEATH

Card Number: 13

The Death card symbolizes a transformation or a dramatic change.

The Death card is one of the most feared and misunderstood cards in the deck. You can relax: it does not indicate a literal, physical death. Something major is coming to an end to make way for something new. Think death and rebirth.

This card might call on you to relinquish old behaviors, drop an unhealthy attitude, depart from a job, or begin a new relationship. Maybe a death-rebirth situation is already under way, and this card is confirming your choices, saying, "You're right on track." This card often invites you to ask: What is coming to an end? What is yearning to be born?

REVERSED

Turn this one upside down and it's all about fear of change, resistance, and a stubborn unwillingness to embrace change or move forward. Getting stuck or bogged down. Putting something off. Hanging on for dear life. Throwing a tantrum because "I liked it the way it was!"

NOTICE THE SYMBOLS

THE WHITE ROSE The white rose is a symbol of transformation and purity.

THE SUNRISE Here comes the sun! The sun rising in the background hints at a new beginning.

THE WHITE HORSE White is the color of purity, and the horse represents movement. This symbolizes the step forward, purification, and the process of moving on.

THE PEOPLE Pay very close attention to the people in this card: a king lies dead, a sign that death comes to all, no matter their status. The pope begs for mercy, while the maiden seems to accept her fate. The child hands the skeleton a rose . . . she welcomes change. Which role do you typically play? How do you deal with change in your life?

COLORS In the Rider Waite deck, the horse is white. The skeleton wears a suit of black armor and carries a black flag with a white rose emblem. He has a red feather in this helmet. The king wears a blue robe, while the pope is clothed in yellow garments. The maiden wears a white dress, and she has a red rose in her blonde hair. The child wears a blue tunic, red tights, and a red garland over her black hair. The sunrise is bright yellow, the river blue, the ground yellow, and the mountains are dark blue.

Which colors signify death, renewal, and rebirth for you?

DEATH.

TEMPERANCE

Card Number: 14

Temperance can symbolize finding "the middle way" between extremes. Seeking the center.

Right on the heels of the dramatic transformation that the Death card offers, we come to Temperance, the card of moderation and balance. The angel in the card transfers water from one cup to another, signifying healing. This action is also related to "blending," as in testing things out to find the right mix.

Going with the flow. Finding the sweet spot. Patience and calm. Sobriety, emotional stability, and spiritual growth. That's what Temperance is all about.

REVERSED

Our sense of balance becomes disrupted. This can lead to extreme behavior, like overdrinking or gluttony. Circumstances spiral out of control, and there is no middle ground to stand on. Things get out of hand. Temperance reversed can also be interpreted as an inability to reach a decision, oftentimes due to "sitting on the fence" rather than taking the right action. Torn between two choices.

NOTICE THE SYMBOLS

FEET The feet of the angel are positioned so that one stands firmly on the banks while the other dips carefully into the pond. This symbolizes the link between the unconscious and the earthly plane. It also suggests "testing the waters" before making a decision.

WATER FLOWING BETWEEN THE CUPS This action symbolizes transformation. Think of a time when you've added a new ingredient to a recipe and that new ingredient suddenly made the whole dish "sing." That's what this is like. Finding that delicious combo. What could you introduce into a situation to make it better?

THE PATH The road represents a journey. But is the angel returning from a journey or preparing to leave?

COLORS In the Rider Waite deck, the angel is dressed in a white robe. His hair is yellow, as is the ornament on his forehead. His wings are red, as is the triangle on his chest, a symbol of alchemy. The cups, crown in the background, and irises are yellow. The water, mountains, and sky are light blue. The grass and leaves are green.

Which colors make you feel balanced and harmonious?

XIV

TEMPERANCE.

THE DEVIL

Card Number: 15

The Devil card represents bondage, addiction, ego, materialism, negativity, fear, being a slave to your desires, or feeling trapped because of choices you've made.

Like the Death card, the Devil tends to be one of the scarier cards in the deck. It's not surprising, considering the fearsome image: two naked people chained to a demon! Have you ever gotten yourself into a hard, dark place where you felt unable to escape? That's the energy of the Devil.

But there's a silver lining here: if you look closely, you'll see that the chains on the human figures are loose. They could escape if they really wanted to. Will you remain chained even though freedom could be yours? Will you remain stuck in place?

REVERSED

Turn the Devil on his head and we find escape from misery! You're taking off the shackles and liberating yourself. The courage to give up your addictions or to face your demons—that's the vibration of the Devil reversed. The end of a bad situation. Recovery or sobriety. Freedom at last!

NOTICE THE SYMBOLS

INVERTED STAR The inverted five-pointed star is a symbol of "the left-hand path" or black magic. This represents being ruled by the ego or unhealthy desires.

CHAINS Chains are symbolic of being bound or restricted in some way (duh, right?). Here, the Devil controls the figures (which could be interpreted as your inner demons).

THE FLAMING TORCH Torches are symbols of illumination. Remember: one match can light a whole room. Should you choose to see, you can find the way out.

COLORS In the Rider Waite deck, the demon figure is orange, and the fur on his legs is brown. The horns and wings are gray, as are the chains. The human figures are peach, and their hair is dark orange. The flame on the torch and the male figure's tail is yellow and orange. The female has a green tail topped with purple grapes. The background and pillar on which the demon stands are both black.

Which colors make you feel negative, restricted, trapped, or stuck?

THE DEVIL .

THE TOWER

Card Number: 16

The message of the Tower is blunt: get ready for destruction and upheaval!

See those figures leaping out of the burning building? Yeah. This isn't a subtle card. The Tower is all about chaos, uncertainty, or a shock to the system. The bolt of lightning represents a sudden, unexpected change that disrupts the foundation and burns things down to the ground. But destruction isn't always a "bad" thing. Sometimes dramatic upheaval is necessary so that we can rebuild a better foundation. Revolution, baby. Things crumble only to be replaced. This card can represent liberation and a new beginning. Sometimes we need a devastating storm to clear the air.

REVERSED

This card still represents "a change in the air," but one that's more gentle and less intense. Think a boss announcing layoffs a few months before they actually happen rather than making a sudden, unexpected announcement. Softening the blow. This reversal can also indicate repression or a refusal to accept a change. Are you stuck in the burning Tower, refusing to budge, even though it's clearly time to get the hell out? Never underestimate the power of denial.

NOTICE THE SYMBOLS

LIGHTNING BOLT The lightning bolt can represent a "wake-up call" or revelation. Think bolt of inspiration.

FIRE Fire is a symbol of destruction and purification. It burns everything clean so that we can rebuild.

CROWN The falling crown represents the crown chakra. As it flies off the top of the Tower, this suggests becoming free from your own ego.

THE FALLING FIGURES These guys are not looking very happy with their predicament. They are fleeing, falling, losing control. But this upheaval could be a "rude awakening" with a silver lining—an opportunity to rebuild and "get it right" this time around.

COLORS In the Rider Waite deck, the tower is gray, and the skies are dark blue. The clouds are dark gray, as is the mountain. The lightning bolt, flames, and crown are yellow, as are the sparks surrounding the tower. The figure on the left has yellow hair, a red cloak, blue tunic, and gray tights and boots. The figure on the right wears a blue robe, red shoes, and has yellow hair and a yellow crown.

Which colors make you feel chaotic or disrupted?

THE TOWER.

THE STAR

Card Number: 17

The Star symbolizes wishes coming true. Hope. Inspiration. Healing.

If you wish upon a Tarot card, this is the one you want to see! It's the calm after the storm. Peace and hope after a crisis. Miraculous rebuilding when all seemed lost. The Star represents the power of belief that keeps us going, no matter what life throws at us. Things may have been rough, but now? All is well.

REVERSED

The hope is lost and pessimism takes its place. "Debbie Downer." Limited options. Wishes delayed or denied completely. Inability to express one's truth. This card can also indicate illness—a stagnation or blockage of some kind. When this card shows up reversed, it's often a signal to adjust your attitude, your lifestyle, or both.

NOTICE THE SYMBOLS

STARS Stars are a symbol of hope and guidance. If you've ever been lost in the woods, you know that the North Star will guide you home.

BIRD Birds are symbols of aspiration. They are also messengers. This bird is an ibis, which can symbolize creativity.

THE VESSELS The maiden in the card pours the water without a care in the world, trusting that the universe is abundant. These vessels can symbolize emotions, and the pouring represents emotions flowing freely.

COLORS In the Rider Waite deck, the background is blue, and the small stars are white. The main star is bright yellow. The figure is peach with yellow hair. The bird and vessels are orange. The grass is green, and the pond is blue. The tree is brown with green leaves, and the flowers have dark green leaves and light purple blossoms.

Which colors make you feel inspired, hopeful, or renewed?

XVII

THE STAR.

THE MOON

Card Number: 18

The Moon signifies a loopy, wild, and emotional ride.

Have you ever experienced a "dark night of the soul"? A moment when the path forward seemed unclear or when nothing made sense anymore? This is the essence of the Moon. Nothing is as it seems. Uncharted territory. Fluctuating circumstances. Illusions. The hottie who asked you out could be guarding a mystery or a secret. The new friend in your circle could have hidden motives. Dreams, imagination, and intuition are also connected to this card. Maybe you are letting your imagination run wild, clouding reality.

REVERSED

Reversed, the Moon can indicate clarity or "seeing the light." Hard times coming to an end. Simplicity replacing complexity. An aha! moment. The mystery has been solved! The Moon reversed can also symbolize the struggle against our animal nature. The Moon, also called Luna, is where the word *lunatic* came from. The Moon reversed can suggest an emotional crisis of some kind—maybe you or someone else is acting totally bonkers, or, depending on your interpretation, maybe the "cray-cray" times are finally coming to an end.

NOTICE THE SYMBOLS

THE CRAYFISH This guy symbolizes our hidden psychic powers as well as our anxieties and fears. Water is often seen as a symbol of the subconscious—so this little critter represents instincts that arise from our subconscious minds as well as irrational fears.

THE DOG AND WOLF These furry fellows represent the dual sides of our minds—the tame side and the wild, instinctual, animal side. Domestic versus primal.

THE TOWERS The two towers represent a choice or a gateway. Which way should you go?

COLORS In the Rider Waite deck, the background, mountains, and water are blue. The towers are white, and the path is light brown. The dog on the left is brown, and the wolf on the right is light brown. The crayfish is dark blue. The moon is yellow.

Which colors make you feel moody, anxious, or dreamy and imaginative?

THE MOON.

THE SUN

Card Number: 19

The Sun represents abundance, prosperity, happiness, and success.
Everything can move forward with ease, joy, and glory.

Here comes the sun, and I say, it's all right," sing the Beatles. That's the essence of this cheery card! One look at the joyful expression on the baby's face, with his arms spread wide, and you know that this is a good omen to see. This card represents optimism and the promise of a new day. Recognition, success, and achievement. The future's so bright, you gotta wear shades.

REVERSED

The reversed Sun still represents happy, cheery energy, but it's muted or somewhat clouded over. Circumstances beyond your control may have diminished the joyfulness of an otherwise happy situation. Or it could be that you are simply unable to see the bright side of a situation. If you've ever had someone "rain on your parade," you know exactly what this reversal feels like.

NOTICE THE SYMBOLS

THE CHILD The baby symbolizes birth or rebirth. The nudity symbolizes the freedom that comes when we feel open and able to express our true selves. Baby, you were born this way.

THE WALL In this card, the wall represents the past or what we are leaving in the dust. Break on through to the other side.

THE SUNFLOWERS Sunflowers turn their faces to the Sun, a reminder to focus on what is bright and positive. Sunny-side up.

THE BANNER A flag or banner symbolizes some sort of announcement. Make way for a happy change!

COLORS In the Rider Waite deck, the child is peach, and his hair is yellow and adorned with yellow flowers. The sun is bright yellow, and the sunflowers are a golden yellow with green leaves. The horse is white, and the banner is bright red. The stone wall is gray.

Which colors make you feel joyful?

THE SUN .

JUDGEMENT

Card Number: 20

The Judgement card represents the possibility of a major change or a personal revelation.

It's Judgement Day! Time to review your life and release whatever's holding you back from reaching the highest heights. The presence of the Judgement card can represent a sign, a nudge from above, a strong pull toward your purpose or calling, or a cosmic "wake-up call" that allows you to finally see the light. Will you heed the call? If you do, you can look forward to enlightenment, renewal, or a happy ending that paves the way for a new beginning. Shed the old life. Rise and shine!

REVERSED

Judgement reversed can indicate a refusal to heed the call. Ignoring the signs that are right in front of your face. A resistance to change or stubbornly holding on to the old ways. Denial or making excuses. This is akin to burying your head in the sand and praying that whatever is "calling" to you right now will just go away. Why won't you rise to the occasion? What are you so afraid of?

NOTICE THE SYMBOLS

THE HORN The horn represents a message, announcement, or call. A wake-up call.

THE CROSS ON THE FLAG The cross can represent the four elements or four directions. It's also a symbol of a crossroads—a time to question which path you might take next.

THE COFFINS No, this isn't a zombie flick, but it is a symbol of the old life that is being abandoned.

COLORS In the Rider Waite deck, the naked figures are gray, and their hair is yellow. The angel Gabriel has yellow hair with orange highlights, and he holds a yellow horn. The wings are light red and gray, and his garment is light blue. The water and sky are also light blue, as are the mountains. The coffins are gray.

Which colors make you feel renewed?

XX

JUDGEMENT.

THE WORLD

Card Number: 21

The World symbolizes the end of a journey.

This is the final card in the Major Arcana. A milestone or important goal has been achieved. Achievement. Success. Integration. A cycle comes to a rewarding end. This is that feeling of joy and accomplishment that comes when you've worked very hard on a goal—a successful culmination of your efforts. Spiritual graduation. A new journey awaits and . . . the world keeps on turning.

REVERSED

The World reversed can indicate a massive setback. Your world is turned upside down, and you may need to go back to the drawing board. Delays. Blocks. A kink in the plans. (If a client asked me about a real estate transaction or business sale and the World reversed showed up, I'd probably say, "Don't pop the champagne just yet.")

The World reversed can also indicate an inability to find closure, move on, or learn from past mistakes. What's holding you back? What do you need to finish or resolve in order to move forward?

NOTICE THE SYMBOLS

THE WREATH Wreaths are a symbol of victory. The woman in the middle of this wreath almost appears to be doing a little victory jig.

THE FOUR FIGURES These are the same four figures as on the Wheel of Fortune card. This represents the balance of the four elements.

THE POSITION OF THE WOMAN'S LEGS Like the Hanged Man, the female figure in this card is crossing one leg at a right angle while keeping the other leg straight. She's standing on her own feet, at a crossroads, and is ready for the next leg of her journey.

COLORS In the Rider Waite deck, the female is peach-colored, and her hair is blonde. Her sash is purple, and she holds two white wands. The wreath is green and tied with a red ribbon. The angel and eagle are yellow, and the ox and lion are brown. The sky is light blue, and the clouds are white.

Which colors make you feel successful and victorious?

THE WORLD.

THE MINOR ARCANA

While the Major Arcana cards represent big, powerful cosmic forces (think destiny, your true calling, intense emotions, crushing defeat, victory, and triumph), the Minor Arcana cards tend to represent your day-to-day life: everyday choices and actions that can help you fulfill your bigger destiny . . . or not.

The Minor Arcana is divided into four suits:
- Cups
- Wands
- Swords
- Pentacles

Each suit is associated with a different element:
- CUPS water
- WANDS fire
- SWORDS air
- PENTACLES earth

Each suit (element) corresponds to different areas of our lives:
- CUPS (water) deal with emotions, love, and relationships.
- WANDS (fire) are connected with enterprise, action, and passion.
- SWORDS (air) deal with intellect, truth, ideas, sorrow, and conflicts.
- PENTACLES (earth) relate to practical matters, work, finances, our physical bodies, and our values.

There are fourteen cards in each Minor Arcana suit—ace, two, three, four, five, six, seven, eight, nine, ten—and four Court cards—Page, Knight, Queen, King. The Minor Arcana represents our day-to-day activities and challenges, while the Courts symbolize the people involved in our lives or the energy we may be bringing to the situation. We'll start with the Minors and then give special attention to the Court cards so you can understand the different personalities of each one.

THE SUIT CARDS

First, let's talk a bit more about numbers and suits. We'll talk more about Court cards and what they mean later.

Each number in the series holds significance.

ACE new beginning, new offering

TWO choice, duality, union

THREE creativity, expression, growth

FOUR stability, foundation

FIVE change, instability, conflict

SIX harmony, balance

SEVEN challenge, struggle

EIGHT achievement, manifestation

NINE ending, completion

TEN the final manifestation or completion, endings and new beginnings, results

When you are interpreting a Minor Arcana card, you want to consider the number of the card (ace, two, three, four, five, and so on) as well as the suit of the card (Cups, Wands, Swords, Pentacles). Combine the number plus the suit to get the full meaning of the card. (It's like Tarot math!)

For example, let's say you are doing a Tarot reading and you pull out the Ace of Pentacles.

- The number is one, otherwise known as ace. The ace card (in any suit) generally represents a new beginning.
- The suit is Pentacles. Pentacles generally represent practical matters, work, and finances.
- Add 'em up!
- Number + suit = full meaning of the card.
- A new beginning + practical matters, work, and finances = a new career or financial opportunity.

So, if a friend asked you, "Would moving to Minneapolis be a good choice for me career-wise?" and the Ace of Pentacles showed up in the reading, you might tell your friend, "Yep, looks like moving there could result in a better job, a pay raise, or some other kind of new financial opportunity."

Here are a few more examples of these number plus suit combos:

FIVE OF CUPS change + emotions = a change of heart

THREE OF WANDS creativity + enterprise = a new creative project or business project

TEN OF SWORDS completion + conflict = the end of a conflict

EIGHT OF PENTACLES achievement + finances = a big financial goal realized

As you color your way through the Minor Arcana, you'll begin to get the hang of this number + suit math dealio.

This may seem complex at first, but over time, you'll memorize all the combinations, you'll remember the associated visuals, and everything will feel very familiar. (Promise!)

Let's start coloring the Minors!

ACE OF CUPS

Element: Water

The Ace of Cups indicates a new emotional beginning.

This card is a good omen to see in a reading, especially regarding matters of love. The hand offers an overflowing cup, a symbolic gesture of giving with an open heart. Are you ready to give as well as receive?

This can be the start of an important relationship or a proposal. It can also symbolize physical, emotional, or spiritual healing. Cups can also be attributed to creativity, so this card could indicate a new creative project. The dove and wafer represent spirituality. Rebirth, renewal, and emotional rebooting. Nourishing the emotional and spiritual body. Flowing into something beautiful and new!

REVERSED

The reversed Ace of Cups represents blocked emotions. The energy no longer flows freely. Self-expression becomes repressed or overly dramatic and unbalanced. Think drama queen! This can also suggest emotional unavailability or unrequited love. In relationships, a fear of getting hurt may be getting in the way. If you cannot trust and approach your partner with an open heart, the relationship may not blossom to its full potential. This reversal can also indicate an inability to give or receive or a creative block.

NOTICE THE SYMBOLS

WATER Go with the flow! Water is a symbol of emotions and cleansing.

THE CUP The Holy Grail. Love in the highest, purest form. No matter what we are approaching, we must operate from a place of love. From there, all things are possible.

THE DOVE The dove is a symbol of peace and healing. It also indicates hope. Are you trusting that what is being offered to you is for your highest good?

THE WAFER In the Catholic religion, the wafer is a symbol of the body of Christ and is consumed during Communion. It represents transformation and connection—the kind that happens when love is met with love.

THE HAND An open hand is a gesture of giving and also receiving. Are you giving and receiving love equally?

THE LOTUS In Buddhist and yogic lore, the lotus is a symbol of growth and renewal. It grows beautiful in the mud, a sign that even difficulties can help us become pure.

COLORS In the Rider Waite deck, the dove and wafer are both white. The cup is a brilliant golden yellow, and the water is sky blue. The lotus leaves are green, and the blossoms are deep pink.

Which colors make you feel flowy, loving, or creative?

ACE of CUPS.

TWO OF CUPS

Element: Water

*The Two of Cups symbolizes the spark or mutual attraction that brings people together,
a strong connection that leads to a loving partnership or deeper understanding.*

The Two of Cups is always a welcome card, especially in readings concerning relationships. But this doesn't always need to be romantic in nature . . . this same emotional engagement can also happen with business partners or family. People coming together or being able to meet halfway. Shared joy.

REVERSED

Turn this card upside down and the connection breaks. Instead of agreement, we find conflict and a lack of cooperation. A negotiation falls apart. A breakup. A split. A once promising union goes bad.

NOTICE THE SYMBOLS

THE COUPLE Notice how they are facing each other in a toast while the male figure reaches a hand toward the female? This gesture represents coming together—whether that be for love, negotiation, or cooperation.

WINGED LION The lion is associated with passion, sexuality, and heart. The wings symbolize the spirit. Love can take flight.

CADUCEUS The Caduceus is the staff carried by Hermes, but it's also used to represent modern health care organizations, making it a symbol of healing. When you combine this with the lion's head, we see the healing forces of love.

COLORS In the Rider Waite deck, the lion head and wings are red. The cups are yellow. The female figure wears a green laurel wreath, white gown, and blue overgarment. The male is wearing a red rose wreath, multicolored tunic, yellow tights, and light brown boots. The hills are green, and the house in the distance has a red roof.

Which colors say "Let's connect" to you?

THREE OF CUPS

Element: Water

The Three of Cups symbolizes joyful gatherings, celebrations, and friendship.
Support. Community.

The playful energy in the Three of Cups suggests fun and merriment. Party time! Here, the three women come together to raise their glasses high in a gesture of celebration. Who is in your inner circle? Is it time to throw a festive shindig?

REVERSED

This card indicates that the party's over. The fun comes to an end, and now it's time to get back to work. The Three of Cups reversed can also symbolize excess—too much of a good thing. Another interpretation may be the disintegration of a group of friends. Shattered friendship bracelets and "mean girl" gossip.

NOTICE THE SYMBOLS

THE FRUITS AND PUMPKIN These are symbols of harvest or abundance. Give thanks for all that you've been given.

WREATHS Wreaths symbolize victory. Time for a victory dance!

COLORS In the Rider Waite deck, the cups are yellow, and the woman to the right wears a white robe and an orange overlay. The one in the middle is clad in a red robe, while the woman on the left wears white. The leaves and grass are green, and the pumpkin is orange. Red and orange fruits peek out from the leaves.

Which colors feel festive and celebratory to you?

FOUR OF CUPS

Element: Water

*The Four of Cups represents discontent or the inability to see
and appreciate the opportunities in front of you.*

The festive energy of the Three of Cups is followed by the somber, apathetic Four of Cups. Here, the figure sits by a tree, arms crossed and a bored expression on his face. He's being offered many options, but he chooses nothing. Is he disinterested? Emotionally unavailable? Is he rejecting an opportunity? Or maybe he just can't see how good the opportunity might be. If there's one Tarot card in the deck that represents the emotional state of "meh . . . ," it's this one.

REVERSED

The reversed Four of Cups is no longer sitting passively. Now it's time to take action and seize the opportunities at hand. Jumping at the chance. Time to get back in the game after a time-out. Have you ever had an offer come out of the blue that was too good to pass up? That's the energy of the Four of Cups reversed.

NOTICE THE SYMBOLS

THE CROSSED ARMS Pay attention to body language in the cards, for they hold clues. The crossed arms indicate stubbornness and a closed-off heart chakra. He's not open to anything that is being offered.

THE HAND EXTENDING THE CUP This is a symbol of a divine gift or the hand of fate. Pay attention to what is being offered!

THE THREE CUPS IN FRONT These symbolize past experiences. Been there, done that.

COLORS In the Rider Waite deck, the cups are yellow, and the figure wears blue tights and a red blouse with a dark green tunic. The grass and leaves are green, while the trunk is light brown. The hand and cloud are both white.

Which colors make you feel apathetic or closed off?

FIVE OF CUPS

Element: Water

In the Tarot world, the number 5 is often a sign of change.
The Cups represent emotions, so the Five of Cups can indicate a "change of heart."

The mourning figure cloaked in black stands staring at three spilled cups. She cannot see the two that are upright behind her. This symbolizes sorrow, heartbreak, loss, and grief.

Whatever has happened, accept the loss. Grief and loss are parts of life that everyone experiences eventually. How we react to that loss is what matters. Is your glass half-empty or half-full?

REVERSED

This card is still difficult, even when reversed, but it holds glimmers of hope. It's possible that there is a new outlook. The loss has been accepted, the water is now under the bridge, and the healing process begins. Forgiveness. Surrender. It's time to move on with what is left.

NOTICE THE SYMBOLS

THE CASTLE The castle can represent a goal or desire. Perhaps the grieving figure is unable to see how to reach his destination? (Hint: stop focusing on what's not working.)

THE BRIDGE A bridge can represent a transition or something that takes us from one place to another. There is a way forward. (Put the water under the bridge and move on.)

THE SPILLED CUPS The three spilled cups indicate past emotional experiences and regret. Crying over spilled milk.

COLORS In the Rider Waite deck, the cups are yellow, and the figure wears a black cloak and green boots. The spilled liquid is red. The river is blue, and the trees and grass are green. The castle is light gray.

Which colors feel connected to grief, loss, or change?

SIX OF CUPS

Element: Water

The Six of Cups is a gentle reminder to pause and enjoy the present moment.

The Six of Cups shows two children standing in a garden setting, one offering the other a flower. It's a reminder that it's possible to find joy through reminiscing about days gone by. Rosy memories from childhood. Happy days of yore. Stop and smell the roses today, but don't forget the path that led you here.

REVERSED

When the Six of Cups is reversed, it can indicate getting hung up on the past. An inability to let go of the old and to see what is right in front of your face. Nostalgia turns to pining for what's already gone. Mourning the old "glory days." It's also possible that you may be looking back and realizing that those good old days weren't so good after all. This can be an invitation to focus on the present and future. Look ahead.

NOTICE THE SYMBOLS

THE HOUSE The houses represent security. There's no place like home!

THE WATCHMAN The watchman seems to be patrolling the garden. What is he keeping in . . . or out? A symbol of protection.

THE FLOWERS IN THE CUP What's blossoming here? The bloom of youth or something growing out of seeds planted long ago.

COLORS In the Rider Waite deck, the cups and ground are yellow. The female figure wears a red hood, a yellow dress with a blue skirt, white gloves, and red boots. The male figure wears a red hood, blue tunic, red tights, and orange boots. The flowers are white with green leaves. The roofs on the buildings are gray, as is the walkway. The watchman wears light blue.

Which colors remind you of a simpler time?

SEVEN OF CUPS

Element: Water

The Seven of Cups represents an inability to make a decision.

Decisions, decisions . . . that's what the Seven of Cups seems to be saying. This is the "kid in the candy store." The beauty of this card is that there are many choices available. Which path should you take when there are so many to choose from? This card can also indicate wishes fulfilled or wishful thinking. The dreamer who builds castles in the sky.

REVERSED

If you reverse the Seven of Cups, it can indicate that the time to hesitate is through. Things are moving forward. A choice might be being made for you, or maybe you will finally find the way to turn your dreams into reality. One way or another, it's lights, camera, action!

NOTICE THE SYMBOLS

THE CUPS If you look closely, you'll see that every cup has a different offering: riches, power, victory, youth, castles, and so on. Some say that these represent the seven deadly sins. What's tempting you at this moment?

THE SHADOWY FIGURE The figure holds out his hand in a gesture that suggests he is taken aback by the choices before him. This symbolizes "being in the dark" and unable to see which way to go.

COLORS In the Rider Waite deck, the cups and snake are yellow. The figure is black. The clouds are white, and the sky is blue. The head, castle, and dragon are blue. The jewels are multicolored. The wreath is green. The covered figure in one of the cups is white with a red aura.

Which colors say "indecisive" to you?

EIGHT OF CUPS

Element: Water

The Eight of Cups represents a new journey or a quest.

Sometimes, you just need to know when to walk. That's the message behind the Eight of Cups. Whether you've had your fill, reached your goal, feel bored, or simply need a change of scenery, the Eight of Cups says it's time to head out. It's time to seek the unknown. Explore. A new path beckons. Wanderlust. This is always a good omen for travel.

REVERSED

The reversed Eight of Cups suggests a return or an inability to leave a situation, even though you should. If you've ever overstayed your welcome or hung on to something (or someone) that you know you've outgrown, then you've felt the energy of the Eight of Cups reversed. In some cases, this reversal can mean the opposite—it can suggest taking off before you're finished.

NOTICE THE SYMBOLS

THE MOON The moon is a symbol of change and cycles. It can also symbolize reflection. If you look inward, what changes might you need to make?

THE STACKED CUPS The neatly stacked cups represent experiences and achievements of the past.

COLORS In the Rider Waite deck, the cups and moon are yellow. The figure wears a red cloak, yellow tights, and red boots. His staff is yellow. The sky and water are blue. The mountains are green.

Which colors beckon you to begin a new journey or make a change?

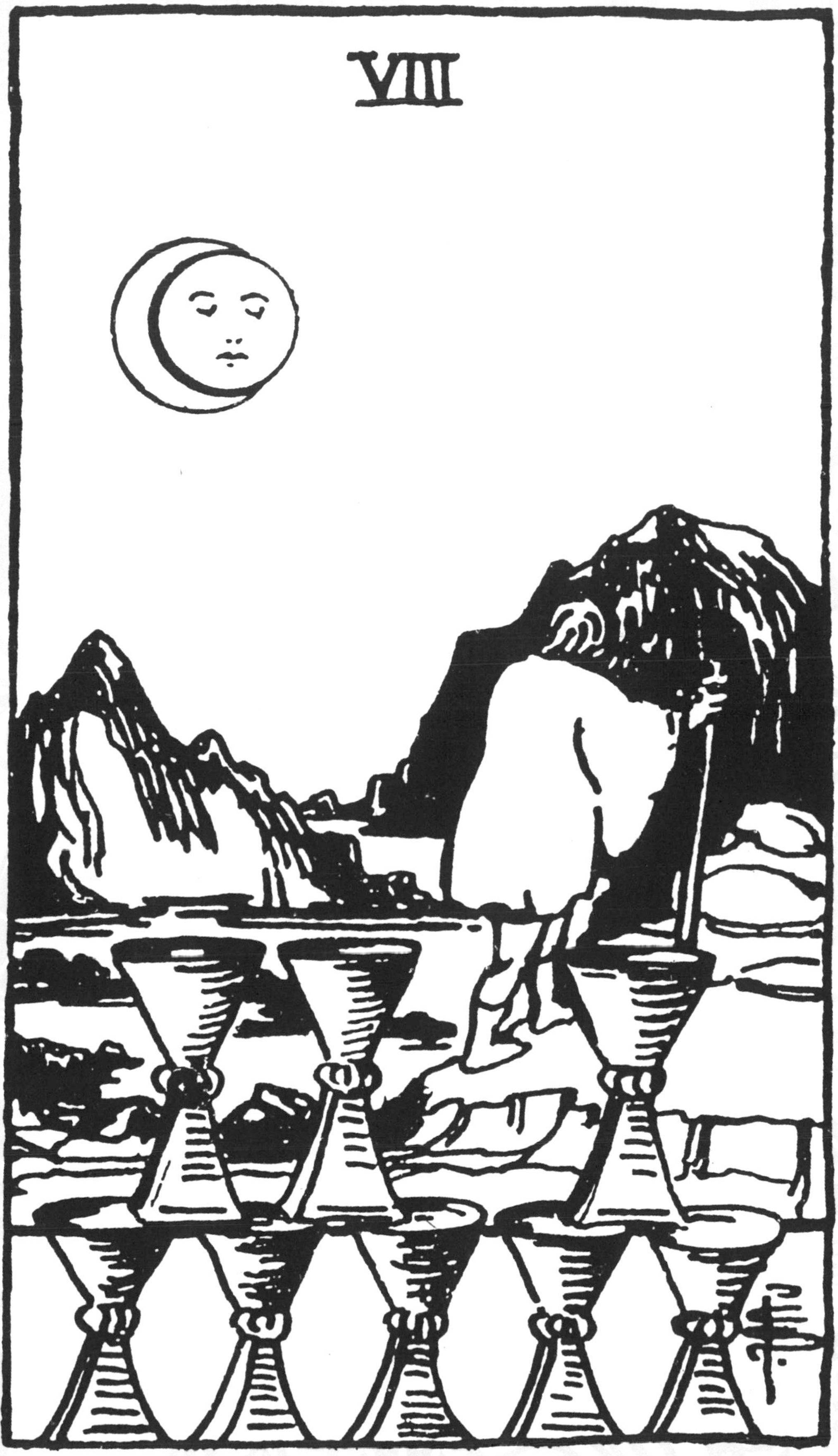
VIII

NINE OF CUPS

Element: Water

The Nine of Cups indicates the fulfillment of wishes or goals.

The Nine of Cups is a happy card to see in a reading, for it's often interpreted as the "wish card." Make a wish! The universe is working very hard on your behalf to grant your wish. This card connotes success at last. The happy results of your actions. Contentment. Pleasure guaranteed.

REVERSED

The Nine of Cups indicates a wish could be delayed or not granted. It can also deliver the old warning: *be careful what you wish for, because you just may get it.* Ever get exactly what you want for Christmas only to realize you'd rather play with the box it came in? Yeah, that. This reversal can also indicate overindulgence or, depending on the nature of the reading, liberation through truth—maybe you're finally being honest about what you want, instead of pretending to share other people's wishes.

NOTICE THE SYMBOLS

THE NINE CUPS LINED UP BEHIND THE FIGURE This represents having everything you could possibly want. Your metaphorical "ducks" are in a row.

THE CROSSED ARMS The crossed arms can symbolize contentment or smugness. He's sitting pretty, and he knows it.

COLORS In the Rider Waite deck, the cups and background are yellow. The cups are on a table with a blue cloth. The figure wears a red hat, white robe, red socks, and brown shoes. He sits on a brown bench.

Which colors represent a wish come true for you?

TEN OF CUPS

Element: Water

*The Ten of Cups indicates the pot of gold at the end of the rainbow
and a joyful conclusion to a long journey.*

If you are seeking a "happily ever after," the Ten of Cups is the card that you definitely want to see! This is the triumphant homecoming card—and an indicator that there is something worth coming home to. Count your blessings because the future is full of promise. This card can represent domestic harmony, contentment, success, and community.

REVERSED

If you reverse the Ten of Cups, the meaning is the opposite: instead of happily ever after, the future looks troublesome. Family quarrels and domestic strife create a drama-filled atmosphere. Dysfunctional family. Divorce. It can also indicate an inability to appreciate all the good that surrounds you. Trouble in paradise.

NOTICE THE SYMBOLS

THE RAINBOW The rainbow is a bridge between heaven and earth and a symbol of blessings. The things you dream of can manifest.

THE DANCING CHILDREN Children can represent innocence and new beginnings. The dancing seems to suggest unbridled joy—the joy of just being a kid, when everything felt possible.

COLORS In the Rider Waite deck, the cups are yellow, and the sky is light blue. The rainbow is red, blue, and yellow. The male figure wears an orange tunic, blue tights, and yellow boots with red trim. The female figure wears a blue dress with a red hem. The child on the left wears an orange dress, and the one on the right wears blue. The grass is green, and the river is blue. The house in the background has a red roof.

Which colors make you feel happy and blessed?

ACE OF WANDS

Element: Fire

*The Ace of Wands represents a new beginning, the turning of a new leaf,
and a sign that things are off to a fabulous start.*

The Ace of Wands is the "thumbs-up" card in the deck. It's a big "Yes!" to whatever you may be asking. Whether you are embarking on a new venture or creative project, or interviewing for a new job, you can take that first step with confidence. All systems are go! The Ace of Wands is also sometimes associated with the birth of a child. If the question is about conceiving, this is the green light to go ahead. In romantic questions, this can indicate the beginning of a passionate relationship!

REVERSED

When the Ace of Wands is reversed, it can indicate a false start. Something begins but never quite gets off the ground. Petering out. An opportunity snatched away. If you've ever started something, only to lose interest or drive, you've experienced the energy of this card. The Ace of Wands reversed can also suggest too much force, desires getting in the way, or a lack of focused effort. This can lead to frustration. Dial it back a bit and gain control. Until then, "thumbs-down."

NOTICE THE SYMBOLS

THE TREES Trees symbolize growth. The seeds you plant now can grow roots. And, apparently, big wands.

THE RIVER The river is a symbol of change and a reminder that things are in motion. Where might this opportunity take you?

THE CASTLE The castle symbolizes security and dominion. Because it sits on a mountain, this castle can also represent a lofty goal. Who wants to be king?

COLORS In the Rider Waite deck, the hand is white, and the clouds and background are light gray. The wand is brown, and the leaves are green. The river is blue. The mountains and trees are green. The castle is light gray.

Which colors feel like a happy start to you?

ACE of WANDS.

TWO OF WANDS

Element: Fire

The Two of Wands represents the achievement of a goal.

A plan coming together . . . beautifully. *Perfecto!* That sums up the Two of Wands. You've got the world in the palm of your hands. Sweet success. But look closely and you'll see that the figure is looking outward, a sign that he's ready to move on to the next thing. When this card comes up in your reading, it may be indicating that you're getting ready to plan your next conquest. This is a card of choices—do you stay and rest on your laurels or go bigger?

REVERSED

The Two of Wands reversed indicates it's action time! No more sitting around plotting world domination—this card calls for jumping right in while the iron is still hot. Change is favored. It's time to go. Hesitation may lead to a lost opportunity. Get out of your comfort zone!

NOTICE THE SYMBOLS

THE WALLS The walls signify security and safety. They can also symbolize boundaries or being "walled in." Will he choose safety or risk?

THE GLOBE The figure holds a little globe in his hand—a sign that he's "got the world in the palm of his hands." The ball is in his court!

COLORS In the traditional Rider Waite deck, the figure wears a red hat and a rust-colored cape over an orange tunic, tights, and boots. His globe is red and blue. The fortress is gray with red and white floral motifs. The wands are brown with green buds. The ocean is blue, and the landscape is green. Small houses with red roofs dot the landscape.

Which colors represent success and achievement to you?

THREE OF WANDS

Element: Fire

The Three of Wands represents new ventures and expansion.

Unlike the figure in the Two of Wands, the man in the Three of Wands card is not content to sit in the castle—he's ready to embark on a journey. It's time to take your plan out into the world with confidence. Some accomplishments are behind you, but there are new opportunities on the horizon. Keep your options open.

The Three of Wands can also indicate that "your ship is sailing in," meaning a reward is at hand. It's also one of the classic cards for travel—especially overseas.

REVERSED

If The Three of Wands turns up reversed, it can indicate a failed expedition. Something you were hoping to accomplish has yet to bear fruit—there is more work and planning to be done. Are you being realistic or trying to achieve something that is out of your reach?

NOTICE THE SYMBOLS

THE SHIPS Ships can signify travel, movement, and risks. What are you embarking on?

THE HILL King of the hill. The hill symbolizes big accomplishments. He's on top!

COLORS In the traditional Rider Waite deck, the figure wears a red robe with a green scarf. His headband is yellow, and his boots are red. The wands are brown with green buds, and he stands on a green and brown hill. The sea is golden, and the sky is yellow. The ships have yellow sails.

Which colors feel expansive to you?

FOUR OF WANDS

Element: Fire

The Four of Wands usually indicates joyful events:
a homecoming, reunion, gathering, or wedding. Rites of passage.

Celebrate good times, c'mon! The festive Four of Wands is a party-on! card. After a hard day's work, it's time to play and celebrate. Kick back and enjoy your rewards. You've crossed the finish line and can claim your reward at last. In a question about love, this card can indicate a stable, committed relationship. Good times for all!

REVERSED

Traditionally, this card is so positive that even reversed, the meanings tend to be the same—but perhaps a little muted. Maybe you feel joyful for no particular reason. Or maybe it drizzles during your picnic—but who cares? Let the party go on . . .

NOTICE THE SYMBOLS

THE GARLAND Garlands and wreaths are often symbols of victory. The hero returns to the cheering of fans! Touchdown!

THE GATE A rite of passage: the four wands form a gate. Gates symbolize passages or new directions.

THE CASTLE A castle can symbolize protection . . . or grand achievements.

COLORS In the traditional Rider Waite deck, the sky is yellow, and the buildings in the background are gray with red turrets. The wands are brown, and the garland has multicolored flowers, purple grapes, and green leaves. There are red ribbons securing the garland to the wands. The figure on the left wears a white gown with a blue shawl, while the other figure has a red shawl. Both figures raise bouquets of multicolored flowers in their hands.

Which colors feel celebratory to you?

FIVE OF WANDS

Element: Fire

The Five of Wands introduces an element of conflict and competition.

Let the games begin! The figures in the card fight it out in a mock battle and jockey for power. The conflict may be exciting and necessary. This is a test of strength and bravado. Sparring or debate. A meeting of the minds. If you've ever worked in an energetic environment that stimulates your ambition, you have tasted the competitive spirit of this card.

REVERSED

The energizing spirit of healthy competition becomes a battleground. Instead of enjoying the game, the Five of Wands reversed indicates a "win at all costs" attitude. Blood sport. Dirty politics and a lack of rules. In some readings, this can represent an inability to hold your own in a conflict or being overpowered by a fiercer competitor. How bad do you want it?

NOTICE THE SYMBOLS

THE BATTLE When you look at this card, you may be struck by the clashing of the wands. This is not violent—the figures are enjoying themselves. This can represent various points of view coming together to create something new.

COLORS In the Rider Waite deck, the sky is blue, and the grass is green. The wands are brown with green buds. The figures wear different-colored tunics: yellow, red, blue with yellow sleeves, blue and white dots, green.

Which colors feel stimulating and exciting?

SIX OF WANDS

Element: Fire

The Six of Wands symbolizes a victory ahead.

The Six of Wands shows a triumphant figure on a horse surrounded by a cheering crowd. The energy is optimistic, as if to suggest an inevitable win. Mission accomplished. An inspirational leader who brings the team to victory. Get ready to step into the winner's circle!

REVERSED

A big winner becomes . . . a humiliated loser. Think the emperor wears no clothes. The reversed Six of Wands symbolizes a fall from grace. This could be a leader who is unable to rally his troops, leading to defeat. Another interpretation might be a betrayal among your peers. Got a lotta enemies? Watch your back. A Trojan horse could be in your midst.

NOTICE THE SYMBOLS

THE WREATHS Wreaths are symbols of victory, and in this card, the figure wears one on his head and also has one tied to his wand. Two for the win!

THE HORSE The horse represents the actions taken or the vehicle that lead to success. Giddyup!

COLORS In the Rider Waite deck, the sky is blue. The figure wears a brown coat over a yellow tunic and orange tights. His boots are orange. The wands are brown. His horse is white and wears a green covering with yellow trim, plus a red bridle and yellow reins. The wreaths are green, and the one on his wand is tied with a red ribbon.

Which colors represent a surefire win or victory for you?

SEVEN OF WANDS

Element: Fire

*The Seven of Wands is the card of courage in action, defense or offense,
and the hard-won victory.*

Conflict arises again—but in the Seven of Wands, the figure fights alone. Think about a time when you felt as if you had to defend your beliefs or fight hard for something you wanted ("me against the world"), and you'll understand the energy of this card. It's all about holding strong and staying on top of your game.

REVERSED

The Seven of Wands collapses under the strain of fighting so hard and becomes weak. The confidence is gone, and cowardice replaces it. Defeat. Indecision. An inability to defend your turf. How will you deal if there is a threat to your position?

NOTICE THE SYMBOLS

THE MISMATCHED FOOTWEAR No foolin'— these mismatched shoes indicate an ability to redirect people's attention or trick people. Perhaps the figure wanted his attackers to assume he had less fight in him than he actually does?

COLORS In the Rider Waite deck, the sky is blue. The figure wears a green tunic over a yellow shirt. His tights are orange, and his boots are brown. The wands are brown with green buds. He stands on a green hill.

Which colors make you feel strong, as if you can stand up and defend your beliefs?

EIGHT OF WANDS

Element: Fire

The Eight of Wands represents swift progress or travel. Momentum at last!

Not a single human figure appears in the Eight of Wands—these wands fly through the air all by themselves. If you look at the direction, they are pointing toward the earth, a sign that something is about to come to a successful conclusion. Something is moving along with great speed. This is a great card to see if you are planning on moving or taking a trip. It is also sometimes associated with important messages. All systems go!

REVERSED

If the Eight of Wands turns up reversed in a reading, it can signify a delay or detour. Things may not be moving in the right direction, or there may be little progress to speak of. The energy is similar to sitting in the car with your wheels spinning—going nowhere fast. This card can also indicate quarrels and conflicts, particularly about a change in the plans, or choosing the right way to proceed.

NOTICE THE SYMBOLS

THE EARTH The earth can indicate grounding or the physical element. Here, the wands suggest joining heaven and earth. Ideas manifesting into something real.

THE RIVER The mighty river in the background represents change and movement. Going with the flow.

COLORS In the Rider Waite deck, the sky is blue. The wands are brown with green buds. The earth is green with a blue river running through it.

Which colors suggest swiftness to you?

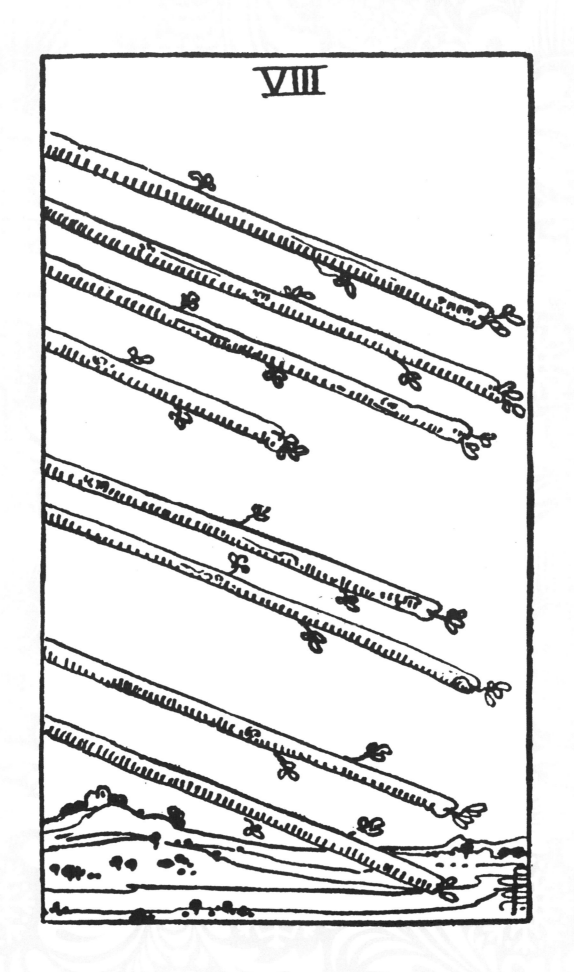

NINE OF WANDS

Element: Fire

The Nine of Wands can indicate a setback before reaching a goal.

The figure in the Nine of Wands wears a bandage over his head, and he looks around warily as he leans on one of the wands. My friend Gillian calls him "the wounded warrior," and this description fits. He's heroic and resolute—standing strong until the end.

You're almost there, but not quite yet. One more test before you're done. Stay on your grind, and don't take your eye off the prize. Guard your turf.

REVERSED

This card can symbolize defeat or giving up. A refusal to engage. Have you ever fought really hard for something only to realize it just wasn't worth it? That's the Nine of Wands reversed. Sometimes this card can also signify a breach of boundaries. Someone is not respecting your space. Shields up! It can also indicate vulnerability. Standing totally naked without any defense.

NOTICE THE SYMBOLS

THE BANDAGE The bandage around his head represents a "psychic wound." What wounds need closure?

COLORS In the Rider Waite deck, the sky is light blue. The wands are brown with green buds. The figure wears an orange tunic, white shirt, yellow tights, brown belt, and green boots. He has a white bandage on his head. There are green mountains in the background, and he stands on a gray stage.

Which colors say "wariness" to you?

TEN OF WANDS

Element: Fire

The Ten of Wands can signify hard labor, oppression, or taking on the weight of the world.

The Ten of Wands shows a man carrying a heavy load of wands. Ahead of him, there is a house. The goal is at hand—victory is in sight—but there is still a little more work to be done. One final push and then you're home free. Although the end is near, the load may feel burdensome. What are you journeying toward? Will it be worth the struggle?

REVERSED

The burden is lifted. Relief at last! Help is at hand, and you no longer have to shoulder the responsibility alone. Sometimes, though, this reversal can indicate a collapse under the heavy weight of your roles and responsibilities. The figure gives up or is forced to abandon his goal. Is it time to just let it go?

NOTICE THE SYMBOLS

THE HOUSE Home sweet home. Houses can symbolize security. The efforts will lead to greater security in the future.

COLORS In the Rider Waite deck, the sky is light blue. The wands are brown with green buds. The figure wears an orange tunic, white shirt, green tights, and brown boots. His hair is blond. There are green mountains and trees, as well as a house with a red roof in the background.

Which colors feel hard or heavy?

ACE OF SWORDS

Element: Air

The Ace of Swords symbolizes truth expressed in the highest form.

The truth shall set you free—and here, the sword cuts through the fog to deliver an important message. This is a mental breakthrough or shift. That aha! moment. The lightbulb goes on, and suddenly you have a brilliant flash of inspiration. A new opportunity that brings fresh mental stimulation. While that all sounds dandy, this card can also indicate the beginning of a conflict—after all, not everybody can handle the truth. Shields up!

REVERSED

The Ace of Swords reversed can indicate mental conflict or confusion. Think losing your grip. Mental discord. The mind is not at rest. Instead of victory and mental stimulation, we find apathy and surrender. An idea that goes nowhere fast. This can also symbolize dishonesty or bending the truth to get your way. In a positive-oriented reading, this card can also signify the end of a battle.

NOTICE THE SYMBOLS

THE CROWN The crown symbolizes the crown chakra, which sits on the top of our heads and connects us to our higher wisdom. The sword piercing the crown indicates breaking through our thoughts and making contact with our higher guidance. Enlightenment, baby.

THE CLOUDS Clouds can symbolize confusion and lack of clarity. Can you look at clouds from both sides now?

THE GOLD SPARKS The six sparks represent consciousness or "the divine spark"—a.k.a. flashes of inspiration!

COLORS In the Rider Waite deck, the hand is white, and the clouds and background are light gray. The sword is silver. The mountains are brown and blue. The crown is yellow, and the leaves are green. The little sparks are yellow.

Which colors represent feeling clear to you?

ACE of SWORDS.

TWO OF SWORDS

Element: Air

Sometimes it's difficult to see which way you need to go—so you sit and refuse to make any decisions. This is the energy behind the Two of Swords.

The figure is blindfolded and seated with two heavy swords balanced perfectly. This is a deliberate, self-chosen time-out. Is it denial? Or just a need to pull back and wait things out until there is a clear path ahead? A solution may not be present. You could be weighing out two equally challenging choices. Wait it out. Meditate.

REVERSED

Either the decision is obvious or someone else is making it for you. The blindfold is ripped off, and reality sinks in. The Two of Swords reversed can symbolize needing to face the harsh truth of a situation. This reversal can also indicate an imbalance. The harmony is lost.

NOTICE THE SYMBOLS

THE BLINDFOLD Third-eye blind. The figure wears a blindfold—why? What is she unwilling or unable to see?

THE ARMS CROSSED OVER THE CHEST Her arms are crossed over the heart chakra, a sign that she's not open. She is choosing to cut herself off or remove herself from a situation.

COLORS In the Rider Waite deck, the sky and body of water are blue. The moon is yellow, and the mountains are brown. The swords are silver. The figure wears a white gown and sits on a gray bench. She is seated on a gray stage.

Which colors feel stagnant to you?

THREE OF SWORDS

Element: Air

With a storm cloud in the background and a heart pierced by three swords,
the Three of Swords represents sorrow, pain, and hurt.

One look at the stark image on this card and it's obvious what it means: heartbreak. A relationship comes to a painful conclusion. Divorce. Accepting the wound is the first step toward healing.

REVERSED

When the Three of Swords is reversed, it's a sign of healing. The storm has passed, and now you can get on with the business of life. Recovery. In some situations, this reversal can symbolize a person who refuses to accept an ending because they do not want to feel the pain. Pushing the pain away or denying it.

NOTICE THE SYMBOLS

THE HEART Hearts generally symbolize our feelings, especially love. Here, that love is being torn apart.

THE RAIN Rain often symbolizes sadness and depression. A downpour of emotions.

COLORS In the Rider Waite deck, the sky and clouds are gray. The swords are silver, and the heart is bright red.

Which colors signify heartbreak or sadness?

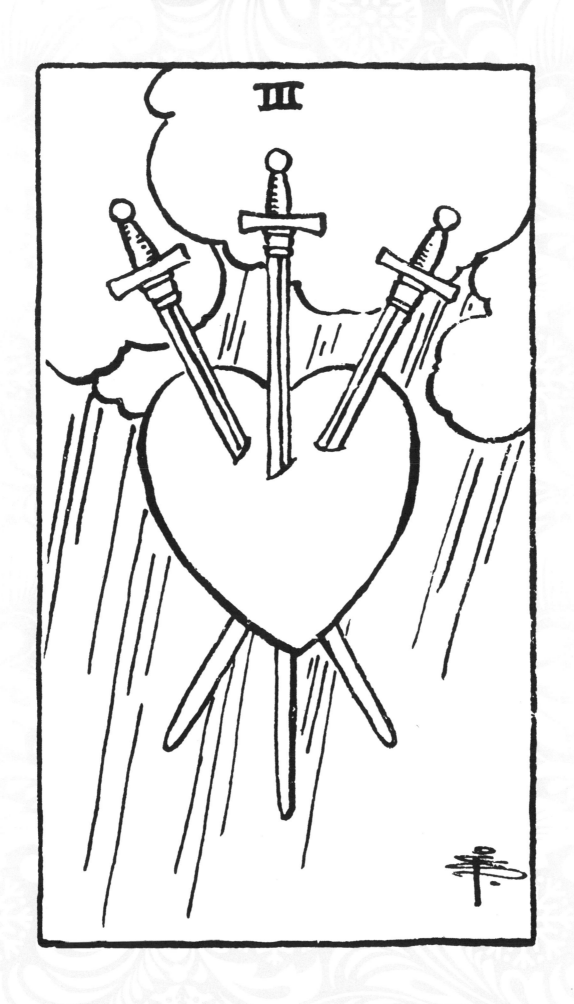

FOUR OF SWORDS

Element: Air

Usually the Four of Swords is interpreted as taking a strategic time-out to heal or plan.

Following the stormy Three of Swords, the peaceful Four of Swords shows a time of rest after a battle. But is the figure really resting—or is this a funeral? In some cases, this can symbolize a stay in a hospital or treatment center, or on a less dramatic note, perhaps retreating to a quiet place to revamp your business plan after an especially busy or stressful quarter. Recuperation. Recalibration. Withdrawal from a situation. Meditation or contemplation.

REVERSED

The Four of Swords is back in action. The time to rest is done. It's back to the grindstone. Time to leave the sanctuary behind and head back into the world, rested and rarin' to go.

NOTICE THE SYMBOLS

THE SWORDS The three swords on the wall represent a painful experience or tough battle, possibly one that's just been completed. The sword in the casket symbolizes "burying" the pain. It's over. Move on.

THE STAINED-GLASS WINDOW If you look very closely, you'll see that the stained-glass window has the word pax ("peace") on it. The stained glass represents perception—this may be a sign that someone is trying to gain a peaceful perspective on a situation.

COLORS In the Rider Waite deck, the walls are gray, and the stained-glass window is multicolored. The swords are silver. The figure and the casket are both yellow.

Which colors feel quiet and contemplative to you?

FIVE OF SWORDS

Element: Air

The Five of Swords can represent winning through deceit or underhanded tactics.

Ominous skies and weeping figures in the distance tell the story of a stormy period and a dubious victory. Defeat, loss, and betrayal. Cruelty. Doing an action with little regard for how it might affect others. Winning by any means necessary. A hostile takeover. To the victor go the spoils, even if he or she doesn't seem to deserve it.

REVERSED

The reversed Five of Swords softens the blow but not by much. This can symbolize healing after a conflict or taking what is left and moving on. A recovery is ahead, even though it may seem impossible right now. This too shall pass.

NOTICE THE SYMBOLS

THE STORMY SKY The dispersing clouds indicate that a storm has passed. This symbolizes a conflict or war that has come to an end.

THE WEEPING FIGURES These two figures symbolize loss, humiliation, and defeat. They have suffered at the hands of the antagonist, who smirks with delight at their pain. Could be a "frenemy" who doesn't really have your best interests at heart.

COLORS In the Rider Waite deck, the sky is gray and stormy. The water is light blue, and the mountains in the background are gray. The figure in the front wears a red shirt covered with a green tunic, red tights, and brown boots. His hair is blond. The figure to the left wears a green shirt, yellow tunic, red cloak, orange tights, and white boots. The distant figure wears all yellow. The swords are silver, and the stage is gray.

Which colors feel ominous to you?

SIX OF SWORDS

Element: Air

The Six of Swords represents the quiet passage or transition through—or following—hardship.

After loss, we must eventually move on. That's what the Six of Swords is all about. The figures in the boat suggest that this is not a lonely journey—there is support to help ease the process. When this card shows up in a reading, it's often a sign that things are slowly getting better. Time for change. Smooth sailing ahead. The Six of Swords can also represent a trip by water. (Caribbean cruise, anyone?)

REVERSED

If you reverse the Six of Swords, it can suggest getting stuck in a rut or revisiting the pain again . . . and again . . . and again. An inability to move forward. Another possible interpretation might be travel problems. Going somewhere? Prepare for delays.

NOTICE THE SYMBOLS

THE WAVY WATER The choppy waves represent movement. Leaving, moving onward, embarking on a new chapter. The waters ahead look smooth as glass—a sign that future will be much easier.

THE FERRYMAN We're in this boat together! A man helps the woman and child by steering the boat. You're not alone . . . help abounds.

COLORS In the Rider Waite deck, the sky is gray, and the water is light blue. The male figure wears a blue shirt with an orange tunic over it. His tights are green, and his boots are brown. The boat is orange. The child wears light purple and has blond hair. The female figure is clothed in a mustard-yellow cloak. The swords are silver.

Which colors make you feel peaceful and hopeful for the future?

SEVEN OF SWORDS

Element: Air

The Seven of Swords indicates cunning or craftiness.

A man appears to be sneaking into a camp and making off with a bundle of swords. Is he getting away with it—or getting caught in the act? This is traditionally the card of theft. It's also a sign of someone acting alone . . . like a stealthy fox entering a henhouse undetected. A hidden agenda.

REVERSED

The Seven of Swords reversed means the stolen goods might be returning home. The theft is discovered, and restitution can happen. Getting caught with your hand in the cookie jar. Time to fess up and make things right.

NOTICE THE SYMBOLS

THE SOLDIERS IN BACKGROUND One has his sword raised. Are they fighting among themselves—or did they discover the thief in the act?

COLORS In the Rider Waite deck, the sky is yellow. The figure is blond and wears a red cap with black trim. His tunic is mustard yellow with red dots. He wears blue tights and red boots with black trim. The ground and stage are light brown. The tents are multicolored. The swords are silver.

Which colors feel sneaky to you?

EIGHT OF SWORDS

Element: Air

The Eight of Swords symbolizes a self-imposed prison—
perhaps an attitude that's holding you back.

All tied up and no place to go—that's what the Eight of Swords seems to say! The figure is wearing a blindfold, and she's restrained with a circle of swords around her. Her feet are free to move, but she cannot see the way out. You've gotten yourself into this predicament, and you may not realize that you can also get yourself out. Liberation can be yours—but first you must go within and ask yourself: How did I get here?

REVERSED

The energy of the Eight of Swords reversed is like taking off a tight corset: ahhh. You can breathe freely. Freedom at last! Whether you are escaping a difficult relationship, leaving a job, or just dropping a negative attitude, this reversal shows that a way out has been found.

NOTICE THE SYMBOLS

THE BINDING The ties that bind. The ropes symbolize an inability to move. Like a Chinese finger trap, the more you struggle, the tighter the binds become. Force may not be the right answer here. To find a way out? Go inward.

COLORS In the Rider Waite deck, the sky and mountain are gray. The figure wears a red dress with a brown undershirt and shoes. The ground is brown with blue pools of water. Her ropes and blindfold are white. The swords are silver. In the background is a gray castle with red roofs.

Which colors represent a feeling of being stuck or bound?

NINE OF SWORDS

Element: Air

One look at the Nine of Swords and it's clear that it represents worry and negative thinking.

The figure sits upright in bed, head in their hands. A situation may be getting worse. Anxiety. Fear. Fretting. Obsessive thinking. Nightmares and sleepless nights. What's keeping you up at night?

REVERSED

When the Nine of Swords is reversed, it symbolizes the end of worry. Things brighten considerably. Waking up from a nightmare and seeing the light at the end of the tunnel. In some cases, this reversal can indicate a refusal to face the problems—delusion, denial—which may make matters worse in the long run.

NOTICE THE SYMBOLS

THE BED Strange bedfellows. Carved into the bed, we see a scene that looks like a duel or fight. The source of worry may be a conflict or betrayal.

COLORS In the Rider Waite deck, the background is black, and the swords are blue. The figure wears a white nightgown and has blond hair. The blanket is a patchwork with a floral motif of yellow and red plus alternating blue squares. The bed is brown with a white sheet and yellow pillow.

Which colors make you feel worried, conflicted, or obsessive?

TEN OF SWORDS

Element: Air

The Ten of Swords symbolizes an ending is at hand.
It may hurt, but there is a new day dawning.

With the dramatic black background and the knives plunged into the back of the figure lying facedown in the earth, the Ten of Swords is a fearsome image to see in a Tarot reading. But look closely—there is a sunrise peeking in the distance, a sign of hope. After a depression, backstabbing, betrayal, loss, or failure, it is time to reboot.

REVERSED

The reversed Ten of Swords symbolizes a new beginning—even more strongly. It's time to get up, brush your shoulders off, and start anew. The worst is over. You've survived. Let go of the pain and start again.

NOTICE THE SYMBOLS

THE KNIVES IN THE BACK The swords are piercing the figure—but there is no bloodshed. This symbolizes the type of pain that comes through the mind, not the physical body. Sometimes we're our own worst enemy, holding on to distress or past injustices far longer than we should.

COLORS In the Rider Waite deck, the background is black with a yellow sunrise. The mountains are gray, and the water is blue. The figure lies on the brown earth. He wears a white shirt with a brown tunic and is covered by a red cloth. His hair is brown. The swords are silver.

Which colors represent a new dawn to you?

ACE OF PENTACLES

Element: Earth

The Ace of Pentacles signifies a new financial opportunity.

Lucky duck! This is one of the most auspicious cards in the deck. The new opportunity could be in the form of a business venture, new job, or a promotion. The seeds of prosperity and security are being planted. This is the card you want to see if you are looking for a new job! Don't be surprised if you receive an offer that leads to greater wealth and security. This could also symbolize the materialization of a cherished goal. Kid, you done good.

REVERSED

The Ace of Pentacles reversed can indicate an opportunity that never quite manifests. For example, this could be the start-up company that can't manage to get off the ground. False starts. A sluggish launch. The beginning of financial problems. A dry spell. A poor investment. This card can also symbolize greed and corruption, as well as lack of responsibility.

NOTICE THE SYMBOLS

THE GARDEN The lush garden symbolizes the potential for growth, while the white lilies indicate purity and new beginnings. Gifts abound. We've got the right conditions for abundance.

THE GARDEN GATE The gateway to higher knowledge. It's not what you have, but what you do with it. How will you treat the gift you are being given?

COLORS In the Rider Waite deck, the hand is white, and the clouds and background are light gray. The pentacle is bright yellow. The grass, gate, and hedges are green. The lilies are white. The path is yellow, and the mountains are blue.

Which colors say "opportunity" to you?

ACE of PENTACLES.

TWO OF PENTACLES

Element: Earth

The Two of Pentacles symbolizes the ability to balance more than one thing at the same time.

The figure in the Two of Pentacles seems to be doing a jig while juggling coins. Think multitasking. Juggling a full-time job while you run your dream business on the side. Raising kids and attending school. Or being "bicoastal." The Two of Pentacles can also represent making decisions, particularly about money. The earth element favors practicality, so this card could be nudging you to make a sensible spending decision. (Groceries, not gold bling or diamond "grillz.")

REVERSED

Imagine trying to juggle two balls—upside down. Impossible, right? That's the Two of Pentacles reversed in a nutshell. This can suggest an inability to manage all of your responsibilities or make a decision. Poor financial moves. Getting overwhelmed. Dropping the ball.

NOTICE THE SYMBOLS

THE SHIPS The little ships in the background can suggest travel. But look closer. The waves are choppy, which suggest learning to navigate ups and downs. This fellow may be discovering how to juggle, multitask, and manage many things at once.

THE INFINITY LOOP The infinity symbol represents unlimited possibilities or potential. He's in the loop!

COLORS In the Rider Waite, the pentacles are yellow. The figure wears red tights, a red hat, a red belt, and a red shirt covered with a brown tunic. The background is light blue, and the water is blue. The ships have yellow and red sails.

Which colors feel a bit unsteady to you?

THREE OF PENTACLES

Element: Earth

The energy of the Three of Pentacles is one of creativity, artistry, and also collaboration.

If there were a Tarot card to represent Michelangelo's painting of the Sistine Chapel, the Three of Pentacles would be it! This is the card for working at a high level, mega talent, and creating amazing things. Teamwork is a beautiful thing. The Three of Pentacles can also point to apprenticeship, someone developing new skills through real-life work experience.

REVERSED

The Three of Pentacles reversed tells a different story: lack of skills, effort, or attention to detail leads to a botched job. Shoddy workmanship. This can also suggest an inability to work well with others. Problems with coworkers or office politics. Sometimes this card can indicate that home repairs are needed soon—just make sure you hire a pro!

NOTICE THE SYMBOLS

THE BENCH Step right up! This bench symbolizes a solid structure or foundation. What gives your work structure?

COLORS In the Rider Waite deck, the temple is gray. The artist stands on a brown bench. He is wearing a yellow apron over a violet tunic with white sleeves. His tights are blue, and he wears violet boots. The monk wears a gray robe, while the other figure wears a yellow cloak and carries a white scroll.

Which colors make you feel creative, artistic, and collaborative?

FOUR OF PENTACLES

Element: Earth

*Four is the number of security, and Pentacles are often associated with money,
which makes the Four of Pentacles a symbol of financial security.*

Yet if you look at the figure, he seems to be holding on to his money as tightly as possible. Is he afraid of losing it? If so, he may choose to hoard his wealth like the Disney character Scrooge McDuck.

This card can sometimes symbolize greed, selfishness, or possessiveness. But there is another meaning here as well: protection. The figure holds a pentacle directly over his heart chakra, which can represent protecting your heart in order to feel safe and secure. We all need boundaries, but how much protection is too much?

REVERSED

This card can indicate a loss or a need to let go. Time to release! When reversed, this card could be urging you to open up, be generous, and give freely. Trust that whatever you give away will come back to you in bigger ways.

NOTICE THE SYMBOLS

THE CITY We built this city on rock 'n' roll . . . or, more likely, practical action and effort. The city scene in the background can represent a community or a world of opportunities. The figure has turned his back on the city—a sign that for now, he's focused on himself.

COLORS In the Rider Waite deck, the sky and ground are both gray. The figure holds gold pentacles. His crown is gold, and he wears a black cape, lined in red over a red robe with blue trim. His shoes are red. The buildings in the city are multicolored.

Which colors represent security to you?

FIVE OF PENTACLES

Element: Earth

The Five of Pentacles can represent material hardship and struggles ahead.

Misfortune has fallen, and times are tough. The bottom has dropped out. That's the vibe of this card. But all is not lost. There is help available, if you are willing to accept it. This card can also indicate feeling like an outsider, or as though you are not good enough or not worthy of assistance. Could you find it within your heart to say, "Please help?"

REVERSED

When the Five of Pentacles is turned upside down, people reach the bottom and begin to climb back up. This is hitting "rock bottom" and finding a light at the end of the tunnel. Accepting help is the first step to getting on your feet again.

NOTICE THE SYMBOLS

THE BELL AROUND THE MAN'S NECK Back in medieval days, lepers often wore bells around their necks to warn people that they were coming. This symbolizes ill health, but also prejudice. Feel as if nobody wants you around? You could be right. Or your negative 'tude could be a self-fulfilling prophecy.

COLORS In the Rider Waite, the sky is black and dotted with white snowflakes. The couple walks on a blanket of white snow. The stained-glass window is multicolored with yellow pentacles. The female wears a ragged orange cloak over a green dress and blue apron. The man wears a green shirt covered with a blue tunic and blue tights. He has a yellow bandage on his foot and a white one on his head. His crutches are brown.

Which colors symbolize poverty or struggle to you?

SIX OF PENTACLES

Element: Earth

The Six of Pentacles is the card of charity, gifts, and generosity.

Remember the troubled times vibe from the last card, the Five of Pentacles? It seems as if the beggars in the Six of Pentacles are finally ready to ask for and receive help. This card can also represent an act of kindness or mercy. Doing the right thing. If you view it from the perspective of the needy people, it can be interpreted as "ain't too proud to beg." Good money karma, coming back around.

REVERSED

The Six of Pentacles reversed can symbolize greed or withholding aid. In some cases, it can represent a refusal to seek or accept help. And on a positive note, it can suggest that help is no longer needed. Maybe it's your turn to be the giver, mentor, or philanthropist now.

NOTICE THE SYMBOLS

THE SCALES The figure holds a scale as he doles out the coins. This is a symbol of justice, fairness, and equality. When we take care of those who are less fortunate, everyone wins.

COLORS In the Rider Waite deck, the sky is gray, as is the foundation the figure stands on. There is a gray building in the backdrop and green trees. The pentacles are yellow. The merchant wears a red hat, coat, tights, and belt. His tunic is blue-and-white striped, and his boots are mustard yellow. The beggar on the left wears a light yellow blanket, while the one on the right wears blue.

Which colors make you feel ready to receive (or give) help?

SEVEN OF PENTACLES

Element: Earth

The Seven of Pentacles symbolizes the rewards and satisfaction that come through hard work.

It's time to get back to work! The figure in Seven of Pentacles leans on his garden tool, pondering what he's accomplished and what is yet to come. Slow growth is good growth. Results are ahead—but the ultimate reward is in the journey itself.

REVERSED

The Seven of Pentacles reversed can suggest an inability to find work—or working for no rewards. It's also a card of impatience—wanting a big payoff before anything has had a chance to fully ripen. As the old saying goes, "A watched pot never boils."

NOTICE THE SYMBOLS

THE GARDEN OF PENTACLES Gardens symbolize growth, and the garden of pentacles is a sign of a profitable harvest. The fruits of your labor.

THE GARDEN TOOL This is a symbol of persistence and hard work that still needs to be done. Work it!

COLORS In the Rider Waite deck, the sky is gray, and the earth is brown. The mountains in the background are gray. The leaves are green, and the pentacles are yellow. The man wears a white shirt with blue sleeves under an orange tunic. His tights are blue, and his boots are orange.

Which colors make you feel ready for a good, honest day's work?

EIGHT OF PENTACLES

Element: Earth

The Eight of Pentacles symbolizes progress.

Have you ever experienced a time when you were enjoying your work so much that you got lost in it . . . only to look up and realize that hours have flown by? That's pure Eight of Pentacles energy. Things are getting done. That desirable "flow state" where creativity channels through you with ease. It's also a card for craftsmanship or learning a new skill. Dedication to the task at hand brings rewards and greater skills.

REVERSED

The Eight of Pentacles card becomes diminished and muted. The quality of your work might feel sloppy or burdened. Flow state? Not so much. The interest is lost and so is the potential. This could represent a feeling of burnout or an urge to drop out of a project or program.

NOTICE THE SYMBOLS

THE HAMMER The figure is hammering away, symbolizing a need to hammer out the details—or get the job done.

COLORS In the Rider Waite deck, the background is gray, and the earth is yellow. There is a gray castle in the back with a red roof. The artist wears a blue shirt and a black apron. His tights are red, and his shoes are brown. He sits on a brown bench and uses a gray hammer with a blue head. The pentacles are yellow and hang on a brown wall.

Which colors make you feel "lost in your work" (in a good way), focused, and productive?

NINE OF PENTACLES

Element: Earth

The Nine of Pentacles represents the rewards that come from doing the work and making the right decisions.

Nine is the number of completion—and here we see a woman standing in a sumptuous garden, admiring the symbols of success that surround her. Luxury, wealth, and independence. This is the moment where you get to enjoy the fruits of your labor. Satisfaction: guaranteed.

REVERSED

If the card is reversed, it becomes a symbol of discontent. That old "grass is greener" on the other side mentality creeps in, and suddenly the contentment is lost. This can also symbolize that the work has not been completed. Unfinished business. An unripe harvest. Time to get back to the field . . . if you want to reap the rewards.

NOTICE THE SYMBOLS

THE HOODED FALCON A bird in the hand is worth two in the bush . . . or, in this case, garden. A hooded falcon symbolizes the discipline that is required to complete projects and reap the rewards.

COLORS In the Rider Waite deck, the background is yellow with brown mountains. A yellow castle with a red roof sits near the mountains. The two trees have green leaves, and the garden is green with purple grapes. The female figure wears a yellow robe with red flowers and trim, as well as a red hat. The glove on her hand is yellow, and the falcon is green with a red hood. The small snail is green. The pentacles are yellow.

Which colors create a feeling of completion and contentment for you?

TEN OF PENTACLES

Element: Earth

This gorgeous card is a happy one to see—
for the Ten of Pentacles symbolizes wealth and security.

The Ten of Pentacles is the "jackpot" card. This could signal a cash windfall or the good fortune of having a solid roof over your head and the love of your family. Magic is all around you. Count your blessings, for they are many. You no longer need to fret about handling basic issues or counting pennies . . . maybe it's time to ask yourself, "How can I give back or share the wealth? What's my legacy?"

REVERSED

Security is lost when this card is reversed. Instead of stability, the energy becomes reckless. This could indicate someone throwing caution to the wind or being tempted by a "get rich quick" scheme. A fortune wasted or lost.

NOTICE THE SYMBOLS

THE ARCHWAY Arches are symbols of harmony and are also a passageway. What new journeys might be ahead?

THE FAMILY Notice that we have a whole generation present: child, parents, an older man. This symbolizes all the stages of life: childhood, midlife, and old age. The complete life journey. Some Tarot readers like to say that the old man also represents Odysseus at the end of his odyssey.

COLORS In the Rider Waite deck, the sky is blue, and the pentacles are yellow. The archway is gray and so are the dogs. The old man has white hair, wears a multicolored robe, and sits on a chair with purple grapes and green leaves. The man on the left wears an orange tunic with a blue shawl, while the woman wears a red robe. The child wears a blue dress and yellow boots. The buildings are orange and brown.

Which colors symbolize legacy and wealth to you?

THE COURT CARDS

Recap:

- There are seventy-eight cards in your Tarot deck.
- Fifty-six of those cards are Minor Arcana cards.
- Minor Arcana cards are divided into four suits.
- Each Minor Arcana suit has fourteen cards in total—ace, two, three, four, five, six, seven, eight, nine, ten—and four Court cards—page, knight, queen, king.

Now we're ready to talk about those Court cards!

In most decks, the Court cards depict human figures—men, women, and children. These figures often represent people in your life, as well as specific opportunities that you are manifesting at this time.

PAGES youthfulness, new seeds, messages

KNIGHTS young men swinging into action, perhaps on a quest

QUEENS feminine power, nurturing energy

KINGS a mature male, masculine leadership, mastery

One important note: with the Court cards—and all of the cards in your Tarot deck, for that matter—try not to get overly fixated on the gender of the figure in the card. Remember that everyone carries both masculine and feminine energy.

For example, getting a knight card doesn't always indicate that a young, action-oriented man is about to show up in your life. A middle-aged woman might possess that same "youthful masculine energy" in her own way.

So if you're doing a Tarot reading and you pull a card depicting a knight (or any other human figure), try not to interpret the image too literally.

Let's start coloring the Court cards!

PAGE OF CUPS

Element: Water

Pages represent young people and youthful energy, and the Page of Cups carries a sensitive, creative, and idealistic energy.

This can be a much-wanted and cherished child who can sense what people are feeling. Pages are often messengers—the Page of Cups could bring a message of love or happy news or a clear intuitive flash of insight. This card can also indicate something new about to begin—like a new relationship or project.

REVERSED

The reversed Page of Cups can indicate immaturity or a refusal to grow up. Peter Pan would be the perfect archetype for the reversal of this card! For messages, this can mean unhappy news or an unwelcome advance. The reversed Page of Cups can also symbolize a lack of imagination or oversensitivity. Ground yourself!

NOTICE THE SYMBOLS

THE FISH Is there something fishy going on here? Hardly. That little fish jumping out of the cup symbolizes ideas and messages arising from the subconscious. Pay attention!

COLORS In the Rider Waite deck, the cups and the stage are yellow, and the water is blue. The figure wears a blue smock with red and white flowers, gold trim, and a red hem over a red shirt. He also wears red tights, golden yellow boots, and a blue hat. The fish is blue.

Which colors say "youthful" and "sweet" to you?

PAGE of CUPS.

KNIGHT OF CUPS

Element: Water

The Knight of Cups symbolizes the dream lover . . . or wearing your heart on your sleeve.

The dreamy Knight of Cups is the romantic, flirty hero who leads with his heart. Think Prince Charming. The ideal sensitive lover. Knights are also action-oriented, and the presence of this card may be urging you to take action based on your feelings. What is your heart telling you? Follow that. This card can represent a romantic or spiritual quest.

REVERSED

The reversed Knight of Cups turns from dream lover to nightmare. Instead of being courtly, this fellow pulls back and turns passive-aggressive. There is a conflict between the head and the heart. An inability to commit or a lack of emotional depth. Possibly even addictive tendencies. If you are receiving an offer, romantic or otherwise, this reversal says to be very clear on what is really being offered before saying yes.

NOTICE THE SYMBOLS

THE WINGS ON HIS HELMET AND FEET These are symbols of Mercury, the messenger and god of eloquence. He is able to express his feelings clearly—and beautifully.

COLORS In the Rider Waite deck, the Knight sits on a white horse and holds a yellow cup in his hand. His armor is silvery blue with red fish and blue streams of water. The wings on his helmet and shoes are blue, as are the reins and bridle on the horse. The mountains are brown, and a blue river runs through them.

Which colors make you feel expressive and action-oriented?

KNIGHT of CUPS.

QUEEN OF CUPS

Element: Water

The Queen of Cups connotes emotional and creative goals realized, emotional intelligence, and healing.

The Queen of Cups is feminine, sensitive, and creative. Naturally psychic, she trusts her feelings in all matters. She is able to focus her will and nurture her dreams. How will you turn your dreams into reality?

REVERSED

The Queen of Cups reversed becomes overly emotional or manipulative—hello, drama queen! This is the type who breaks down sobbing in order to get what she wants. She cannot be trusted. Her emotions are either all over the place or completely blocked. Lack of compassion or empathy. The female lead in *Fatal Attraction* might be a perfect representation of this card reversed.

NOTICE THE SYMBOLS

THE CHERUBS AND SEA NYMPHS ON THE THRONE She talks to angels. Those sweet little cherubs suggest a connection with the spirit world and her subconscious.

THE FANCY CUP Unlike the other Court cards in the Cups suit, the Queen has an ornate cup in her possession. This symbolizes spiritual wealth. In terms of psychic and spiritual wisdom, this chick is "blinged out."

COLORS In the Rider Waite deck, the Queen sits on a gray throne. She wears a white gown and a blue and white robe with red trim. Her crown and cup are golden yellow. Her hair is blonde. The mountains are yellow with green grass. The sea is blue, and there are multicolored stones at her feet.

Which colors represent sensitivity for you?

QUEEN of CUPS.

KING OF CUPS

Element: Water

The King of Cups can indicate mature love or commitment.
It can represent leading with the heart.

Let love rule. The King of Cups has mastered his emotions and leads with love. He's kind, generous, and cares deeply. He provides unconditional love for his family. Although sensitive, he may choose to suppress his own emotions if he feels that it serves the situation.

REVERSED

The King of Cups loses his footing and drowns in a sea of his own making. This can show up as the clingy, manipulative partner who cannot get a grip on his emotions. Deception and swindling are also possibilities. The King of Cups reversed can be emotionally unstable with a tendency toward addictive behaviors. A rude, immature dude.

NOTICE THE SYMBOLS

THE SHIP Land ho! The ship symbolizes a journey. Where do you want to go? You can go as far as your imagination will take you. This ship is also a symbol of navigating a sea of emotions.

THE LEAPING FISH See that fish photobombing the card? Fish represent the subconscious and emotions. This is a reminder that the King's emotional and spiritual energy is always in the background, guiding everything he does.

COLORS In the Rider Waite deck, the King sits on a gray throne. He wears a blue gown with a yellow robe and red trim. His crown is yellow with red trim and blue ear coverings. His slippers are yellow. His cup and scepter are both yellow. The water is blue, as is the fish. The ship is red.

Which colors represent emotional intelligence or mastery to you?

KING of CUPS.

PAGE OF WANDS

Element: Fire

The Page of Wands signifies a youthful, impulsive, passionate, and creative nature. Dynamic and high energy!

The Page of Wands is an adventurous youth and a high achiever. Bold and enthusiastic, he loves a risk. A page can also represent a message, and this fiery fellow suggests a message about a new creative venture or a hot note from a lover (sexting!). Pages also symbolize new beginnings, such as a new project or job. All in all: this looks like good news.

REVERSED

When this card turns up reversed, the child becomes rebellious and prone to rash decisions. Think rebel without a cause. A lack of maturity or confidence could be another possibility. This can also symbolize bad news. Something you were waiting on doesn't pan out. In some readings, this card can indicate an unfaithful partner. Are you seeing the red flags—or ignoring the message because it's not the one you want?

NOTICE THE SYMBOLS

THE SALAMANDERS Lizards and salamanders indicate renewal. Legends say that salamanders can pass through fire without being harmed. Light my fire!

COLORS In the Rider Waite deck, the figure stands on barren land that is brown. He holds a brown wand with green buds. His cloak is yellow with black salamanders. His tights are orange. He wears yellow boots and a white hat with a red feather. His hair is reddish.

Which colors signify a fiery, passionate message or a new venture to you?

PAGE of WANDS.

KNIGHT OF WANDS

Element: Fire

The fiery Knight of Wands tends to be intense, restless, and charismatic.

Knights are action-oriented, and this one seems headed off for an adventure. This guy could be a touch arrogant and definitely full of bravado. If you're asking a question about whether to move forward or not, this card says, "Go for it!" Ride on with confidence and enthusiasm—but keep your feet on the ground so that you don't burn out. Take the risk. Seek adventure. Bust a bold move.

REVERSED

If The Knight of Wands shows up reversed, it can indicate that the person is not ready for the challenges before her or him. Inexperience leads to a fall. Confidence is dashed, and things fall apart. This card can symbolize a situation that gets off to a brilliant start only to burn out and fade away. An unfinished job. The Knight of Wands reversed can also suggest a jealous nature—or a hot-tempered person who is ruled by his or her passions.

NOTICE THE SYMBOLS

THE RED PLUMES ON HIS HELMET AND ARMOR Red can be a symbol of power or passion. The plumes suggest movement. He's being led by his desires.

COLORS In the Rider Waite deck, the Knight sits on a brown horse, and the reins are green. He holds a brown wand with green buds. His armor is silver, and his gloves and plumes are red. His tunic is yellow with black salamanders. The earth is yellow.

Which colors suggest boldness and valor to you?

KNIGHT of WANDS.

QUEEN OF WANDS

Element: Fire

*Queens nurture and lead, and the Queen of Wands is the generous
and honest female leader who loves to be in the spotlight.*

The Queen of Wands sits with her legs wide open and a black cat at her feet—she's confident and comfortable. She appreciates the simple things and loves her life. Her energy is sexual and candid. What you see is what you get—she is not shy about being herself! (Think the bold lead singer of an all-girl band.) This card can be a reminder to nurture your creative fire.

REVERSED

The reversed Queen of Wands becomes domineering and melodramatic. This is the "queen bee" who will stop at nothing to get her way. Jealousy and bitterness are possible. She's temperamental and flighty—she may be helpful, but only to a point. When the going gets tough, she gets going.

NOTICE THE SYMBOLS

THE BLACK CAT He's not bad luck! The black cat is a stoic companion, perhaps the Queen's "familiar." He symbolizes protection.

LIONS These are no cowardly lions! They symbolize courage and power.

THE NEVER-ENDING THRONE Notice how there's no top on the Queen's throne—it extends past the upper edge of the image, and there's no telling where it ends. This gal has limitless potential.

COLORS In the Rider Waite deck, the Queen sits on an ornate orange throne with red lion motifs and yellow armrests. Her crown and gown are yellow, and she has a white robe covering her. She holds a brown wand in one hand and a yellow sunflower with green leaves and a brown middle in the other. At her feet is a black cat. The mountains behind her are yellow.

Which colors make you feel confident, eager to step into the spotlight, and full of potential?

QUEEN of WANDS.

KING OF WANDS

Element: Fire

The King of Wands is honest, straightforward, entrepreneurial, and confident to the core.

Kings indicate mastery and authority. This King is a passionate leader who motivates others into action. If you've ever experienced the charisma of a fire-and-brimstone preacher or a motivational speaker like Tony Robbins, you have felt this card's burning intensity. If anyone can do it, the King of Wands can—and he wants you to succeed, too.

REVERSED

When we reverse the King of Wands, he loses his momentum and sputters out. He may decide that he doesn't want to hold so much responsibility after all. His fire is extinguished, and his attitude turns quick-tempered and impatient. This reversal can also indicate someone with dictator-like tendencies. An egomaniac with a "God complex." Power in the wrong hands.

NOTICE THE SYMBOLS

THE LIONS ON HIS THRONE AND NECKLACE The noble lion signifies leadership and courage. King of the jungle? Indeed.

THE SALAMANDER Salamanders symbolize renewal and alchemy. What is he transforming?

COLORS In the Rider Waite deck, the King of Wands sits on an ornate gold throne with black lion motifs. His crown is yellow with red ear coverings, and his necklace is yellow. He wears an orange gown with yellow trim at the cuffs, a green cowl, and a yellow cloak with black salamanders. He holds a brown wand with green buds, and his shoes are green. The foundation of his throne is gray, and the salamander is green. The earth is brown.

Which colors make you feel like a strong leader, someone who could motivate others?

KING of WANDS

PAGE OF SWORDS

Element: Air

The Page of Swords can symbolize a need to be alert.

En garde! The young Page of Swords stands in a defensive position, as if he's ready to strike. Pay attention. Do your due diligence and gather information. Important news might be coming in. This card may herald the solution to a problem. If this card represents a young person, it may be an intelligent youth who tends to be curious about the world and is quite independent.

REVERSED

The Page of Swords becomes hasty and impulsive. This could mean someone is jumping to conclusions or thinking the worst. It can also symbolize being unprepared for a conflict. Do not engage in a battle of wits if you come unarmed. If this symbolizes a young person, it can suggest one who is immature, thoughtless, or even cruel.

NOTICE THE SYMBOLS

THE POSTURE Notice the young Page's body language. He seems to be standing as if he's getting ready to strike. This is a symbol of defense and preparation. What is he about to do?

THE CLOUDS The Page stands before parting clouds. This symbolizes a breath of fresh air or communication that clears the air.

COLORS In the Rider Waite deck, the background is blue with billowy white clouds. The mountains are blue, and the hill that the Page stands on is green. The figure wears a purple tunic with white trim and yellow sleeves. His tights are yellow, and his boots are red. A black belt circles his waist. His hair is brown. The sword is silver.

Which colors make you feel armed and ready for action?

PAGE of SWORDS.

KNIGHT OF SWORDS

Element: Air

If you've ever had to step into a challenge and confront an injustice,
you've channeled the energy of the Knight of Swords.

Need a hero? The Knight of Swords is the classic knight in shining armor, moving through the storm with sword drawn, ready to fight . . . or to defend someone's honor! The Knight of Swords loves a good challenge. The energy of this mighty card is assertive, direct, and candid. This card can indicate the need to make a hasty decision without hesitation. No hemming and hawing. Onward!

REVERSED

When the Knight of Swords is reversed, he loses his momentum. This can represent someone who is full of "hot air" (all talk, no action) or being dishonest. The assertiveness turns ugly and violent—or impotent. If this card turns up in a reading, it's best to refrain from taking immediate action. Caution and patience are advised.

NOTICE THE SYMBOLS

THE STORM Trouble brewing. Clouds can symbolize confusion or conflict.

THE BIRDS ON THE KNIGHT'S CAPE AND THE HORSE'S HARNESS Put a bird on it! The Swords suit is connected with the element of air, and with these birdies, we've got . . . more air. A whirlwind of activity. This guy is ready to fly!

COLORS In the Rider Waite deck, the background is blue with jagged white clouds. The mountains are brown and yellow. The horse is white with a blue bridle, blue saddle, and blue harness decorated with yellow butterflies and red birds. The Knight wears blue armor with a red feather in his helmet. His cape and gloves are red. The sword is silver.

Which colors make you feel inspired to take action?

KNIGHT *of* SWORDS .

QUEEN OF SWORDS

Element: Air

The Queen of Swords is the cool, logical Queen who never loses her head.
She is concerned with truth and justice, above all.

This is the wise woman who rules with rationality. The female thought-leader, visionary, or judge. Sometimes this card is interpreted as a widow or a woman who has tasted the sorrow of loss. She's professional and career-oriented, a perfectionist with a big vision. This Queen invites you to nurture your ideas. Be smart. Use your head.

REVERSED

The Queen of Swords reversed can symbolize cruelty and bitterness. Someone who's cold and manipulative. This could represent a backstabber or malicious gossip. Someone with the inability to understand people's feelings. An "ice queen."

NOTICE THE SYMBOLS

THE SWORD This Queen is holding her sword upright. She's concerned with truth and justice for all.

COLORS In the Rider Waite deck, the background is blue with fluffy white clouds. The mountains are brown and red. The Queen sits on a gray throne. She wears a white robe with red tassels on the sleeves and a blue cloak decorated with white clouds and red trim. Her crown is yellow with a red scarf. The sword is silver.

Which colors make you feel thoughtful, truthful, fair, and just?

QUEEN of SWORDS.

KING OF SWORDS

Element: Air

The King of Swords is a stern guy—but he's always fair.
Like the other members of the swords court, he's concerned with justice and truth.

His energy tends to be intellectual and authoritative. He's often seen as a thought-leader, boss, or a professional male. A true pro, he has the experience to get the job done right. This card can indicate mastery of the mind. A logical Mr. Spock type who makes his decisions through reasoning, not emotions.

REVERSED

No more Mr. Nice Guy. If you reverse the King of Swords, he becomes a powermonger who will do whatever it takes to bend circumstances to suit his will. Corruption. Zero integrity. He acts without scruples or concern for the law. Could be a white-collar criminal or a tyrant. The hostile boss from hell or the abusive father. Yikes.

NOTICE THE SYMBOLS

THE BUTTERFLIES Butterflies are symbols of transformation and the air element. He's an agent of change.

THE THRONE EXTENDING TO THE SKY
This represents the connection between heaven and earth. He is channeling divine wisdom and perfect logic.

COLORS In the Rider Waite deck, the background is blue with white clouds. The mountains are blue. The King sits on a gray throne, which rests on a brown mountain with green grass. He wears a blue gown with red sleeves and a dark gray cloak. His crown is yellow, and his shoes and cowl are red. The sword is silver.

Which colors represent a just ruler or a trustworthy father figure to you?

KING of SWORDS.

PAGE OF PENTACLES

Element: Earth

The Page of Pentacles is the messenger who brings news of money and good fortune.

This could be a promotion or raise, a financial deal that finally goes through, a job offer, or a business venture that gets the thumbs-up. If this card is representing a person, it's a young, studious type who is focused, methodical, obedient, and dedicated to his craft. The straight-A pupil who brings home rewards and makes Mama proud.

REVERSED

If this card is reversed, it can indicate unwelcome news about money. If you've ever received an unexpected bill in the mail, you've experienced reversed Page of Pentacles energy. This reversal can also symbolize a lack of focus or direction. Confusion about your goals and priorities. Perhaps spreading your energy too thinly. For a person, this could symbolize someone who is impractical and irresponsible.

NOTICE THE SYMBOLS

THE MEADOW The open field shows possibilities for greater growth. Opportunities are wide open.

COLORS In the Rider Waite deck, the sky is yellow, and the trees and grass are green. The mountains in the background are blue. The Page wears an orange shirt with a green tunic and orange belt. His hat is red. His tights and boots are orange.

Which colors signify happy news to you?

PAGE of PENTACLES.

KNIGHT OF PENTACLES

Element: Earth

The Knight of Pentacles suggests that diligent work and a methodical approach are the keys to greater growth.

While knights usually appear to be action-oriented and ready to leap into motion, the Knight of Pentacles stands still, gazing ahead with a freshly plowed field as his backdrop. The field represents the hard work already completed. This practical knight is pausing to consider his next move. This pragmatic energy may be what is needed at this time. Strong and steady win the race.

REVERSED

When the Knight of Pentacles is reversed, his energy becomes scattered. He's unable to get things done and may become stagnant. Stubbornness gets in the way. Like the Page of Pentacles, when this card is reversed, focus is lost.

NOTICE THE SYMBOLS

THE PLOWED FIELD Did you notice that the Page of Pentacles stands in an open meadow? Now with the Knight—the next card in the sequence—we see progress. The field has been tilled. Seeds are ready to be planted. The field shows the promise of fruitfulness.

COLORS In the Rider Waite deck, the sky is yellow, and the trees and earth are brown with patches of green. The mountains in the background are light blue. The Knight wears blue armor with a green plume in his helmet. A red cloth covers his armor. His saddle is orange. The bridle and harness are red. The horse is black, and the pentacle is yellow.

Which colors inspire you to be thoughtful and reflect before acting?

KNIGHT of PENTACLES.

QUEEN OF PENTACLES

Element: Earth

The Queen of Pentacles symbolizes material success and abundance.

She can bring home the bacon . . . and fry it up in a pan. The Queen of Pentacles is the caring, reliable woman who takes a practical approach to any and all situations. This is the "earth mother" who creates security for herself and those in her care. She is fond of material pleasures in life and has business acumen. She trusts herself—and you can, too. She's got it goin' on!

REVERSED

If you reverse the Queen of Pentacles, she loses her luster and has trouble trusting the world . . . or herself. Her energy becomes clingy, scared, and unfocused. The cupboards are bare (at least in her mind), and confidence is replaced with insecurity. When reversed, this card can indicate lack of success, possessiveness, and the dark side of materialism.

NOTICE THE SYMBOLS

THE RABBIT This little hare is a symbol of sexual fertility, making this card a sign of possible pregnancy or some other form of "abundance."

COLORS In the Rider Waite deck, the sky is yellow. The earth is brown with patches of green. The mountains in the background are light blue. Green trees and vegetation dot the landscape. Red flowers surround the Queen. A blue river runs through the background. A small brown rabbit sits to the right. The Queen wears a yellow crown with red decorations. Her hair is black, and she has a green cape. Her shirt is white, and her dress is red, as are her shoes. The pentacle is yellow, and her throne is gray.

Which colors make you feel rich, abundant, and secure?

QUEEN ofPENTACLES

KING OF PENTACLES

Element: Earth

The King of Pentacles is the "master of the coin" and a symbol of material success.

This is the stable, down-to-earth man who provides well for his family. The King of Pentacles is confident and secure. He's protective and benevolent. Think Father knows best. This card could be interpreted as a successful businessman, mogul, or boss. Wealth and stability. Mastery of finances. (You definitely want this guy as your CFO or accountant.)

REVERSED

The reversed King of Pentacles can suggest failure or a corrupt ruler. He's unable to provide—or doesn't want to. Think deadbeat dad. If this is a businessman or politician, he's going to have one question on his mind: "What is in it for me?" When reversed, this card can represent a person who is willing to use whatever financial means possible to get his way, even if it means breaking the law or accepting a bribe. Bad business mojo.

NOTICE THE SYMBOLS

THE SCEPTER This gold scepter is a sign of his authority and rulership. Like a boss!

VINES, GRAPES, AND FLOWERS He's got all the goods! Plants flower around the King's throne, suggesting material wealth, comfort, and luxury. This guy is flying first class.

COLORS In the Rider Waite deck, the sky is yellow, and the mountains are blue. The castle is gray with red and blue roofs. The wall is gray. The king sits on a black throne with gray bulls'-head decorations on the armrests and mustard-yellow ones at the headrest. The King wears a yellow crown with red decorations. His cowl is red, and his robe is black, decorated with green leaves, purple grapes, and orange trim. His armor is blue. In his hands he holds a yellow scepter and pentacle. Red flowers are on the left, while grapevines with purple grapes and green leaves surround his throne. His foot rests on a gray stone carved like a bull.

Which colors make you feel like a sturdy provider and affluent leader, able to support yourself and others?

KING of PENTACLES.

TAROT TO GO—
QUICK INTERPRETATIONS

You've colored your way through the entire deck—all seventy-eight cards—and wowza! It's a lot to remember. I know. Good news: here's a cheat sheet to help you remember what all the cards signify. If you're working with your Tarot deck and you want to jog your memory at any point, just refer to these handy lists:

MAJOR ARCANA

FOOL A fresh start, the beginning of a journey

MAGICIAN Developing skills and talent, manifesting

HIGH PRIESTESS Intuition, trust your gut

EMPRESS Creativity, pregnancy, mother, pleasure

EMPEROR Stability, authority, father, work

HIEROPHANT Conformity, spiritual leader, teacher, or mentor

LOVERS Romance, partnerships, choices

CHARIOT Triumph, finding direction, control

STRENGTH Inner strength, handling problems

HERMIT Turning inward, withdrawal

WHEEL OF FORTUNE Change, luck, karma

JUSTICE Fairness, court or legal issues, balancing the karmic scales

HANGED MAN Sacrifice, a period of waiting

DEATH Transformation, out with the old, in with the new

TEMPERANCE Balance, middle way, choosing carefully

DEVIL Negativity, poor choices, addiction, being stuck

TOWER Disruption, chaos, difficult change, a fall from grace

STAR Hope, optimism, happiness, and health

MOON Danger, fear, lack of clarity, need to reflect

SUN Joy, happiness, abundance

JUDGEMENT Higher calling, awakening, rebirth

WORLD Completion, success, end of an important cycle, graduation

MINOR ARCANA: SUIT CARDS

ACE OF CUPS New love

TWO OF CUPS Romance, meeting

THREE OF CUPS Fun and friends, celebration

FOUR OF CUPS Boredom, apathy

FIVE OF CUPS Loss and grief

SIX OF CUPS Nostalgia, romance

SEVEN OF CUPS Choices, daydreams

EIGHT OF CUPS Moving on, travel

NINE OF CUPS Wish fulfillment

TEN OF CUPS Love and support, family harmony

ACE OF WANDS New job or creative beginning

TWO OF WANDS Making plans

THREE OF WANDS Success or travel

FOUR OF WANDS Security and happiness

FIVE OF WANDS Competition

SIX OF WANDS Success and leadership

SEVEN OF WANDS Challenge

EIGHT OF WANDS Quick movement, travel, news

NINE OF WANDS Caution, boundaries

TEN OF WANDS Hard work, burdens

ACE OF SWORDS A new challenge, mental endeavor, or breakthrough

TWO OF SWORDS Indecision, contemplation

THREE OF SWORDS Heartache, separation

FOUR OF SWORDS Rest after a battle, meditation

FIVE OF SWORDS Victory through deceit

SIX OF SWORDS Moving forward

SEVEN OF SWORDS Thievery, dishonesty

EIGHT OF SWORDS Feeling stuck

NINE OF SWORDS Worry, losing sleep

TEN OF SWORDS Loss, an ending

ACE OF PENTACLES A new financial opportunity

TWO OF PENTACLES Juggling resources, financial decisions

THREE OF PENTACLES Recognition for talent, collaboration

FOUR OF PENTACLES Financial stability, possessiveness

FIVE OF PENTACLES Financial loss, abandonment, poverty consciousness

SIX OF PENTACLES Generosity, charity

SEVEN OF PENTACLES Hard work ahead, slow growth

EIGHT OF PENTACLES Rewarding work, getting lost in a task

NINE OF PENTACLES Financial security, abundance

TEN OF PENTACLES Financial success, legacy

MINOR ARCANA: COURT CARDS

PAGE OF CUPS Romantic message, a well-loved child

KNIGHT OF CUPS A sensitive young male

QUEEN OF CUPS A kind woman

KING OF CUPS A caring man

PAGE OF WANDS Good news, student

KNIGHT OF WANDS An industrious young man

QUEEN OF WANDS A creative woman

KING OF WANDS A powerful man

PAGE OF SWORDS Strong-minded youth, legal news

KNIGHT OF SWORDS A challenging man who enters your life quickly

QUEEN OF SWORDS A rational woman

KING OF SWORDS A logical and intelligent man

PAGE OF PENTACLES A message about money, good student

KNIGHT OF PENTACLES A stable, dependable young male

QUEEN OF PENTACLES A grounded, earthy female

KING OF PENTACLES A secure and successful male

HOW TO COME UP WITH A "GOOD" TAROT QUESTION

To do a good, clear Tarot reading, you need to start with a good, clear question. Let's talk a bit more about how to do that.

Some questions "work" for Tarot and others, not so much. You'll definitely want to avoid asking a yes-no question. Keep it open.

Also try to avoid "Will I . . . ?" questions (like "Will I be offered a book deal this week?") because with that type of question, you are putting yourself in a position where you are being passive about your future. Tarot is not a passive tool. While Tarot can predict likely outcomes and illuminate which choices might be best for you, it's not a guarantee of specific results or rewards.

Here are a few examples of excellent, Tarot-friendly questions:

What can I do to improve _____?

What is the most likely outcome if I choose _____?

What do I need to know about _____?

What is the best way to _____?

How can I get past _____?

What's the lesson I am not seeing clearly when it comes to _____?

Why does _____ keep repeating or showing up in my life?

How can I make the best possible use of my time today?

How can I get motivated to _____?

What is the best way to improve my relationship with _____?

How can I understand _____?

What do I need to know about my relationship with _____?

What should I be focusing on right now when it comes to _____?

What can I expect if I launch my product in [month] versus [other month]?

How can I help _____ to reach her goals right now?

How can I best support _____ at this time?

Why do I have a funny feeling about _____?

I have a great feeling about _____. Is my hunch correct?

What's the hidden opportunity with [situation]?

SPREADS AND LAYOUTS

ow that you're feeling acquainted with all the cards in your deck—from the Fool all the way to the King of Pentacles—it's time to learn how to use your deck to answer your burning questions, compare options, and solve problems.

It's time to spread the cards and start interpreting!

In Tarot circles, you will often hear people talking about a "doing a spread" or "pulling a spread" or "laying out a spread." A "spread" refers to a selection of cards arranged in a particular way. A spread might include one card, two cards, or a whole mess of cards, depending on the purpose of the spread. You can go buck-wild memorizing all kinds of complex spreads. (If you are a Tarot geek like me, it's superfun!)

For total beginners, I recommend starting with a simple one-card spread.

HOW TO DO A ONE-CARD SPREAD

A one-card spread is foolproof. Here's how to do it:
1. Come up with a question.
2. Take a deep breath.
3. Shuffle your deck.
4. Cut the deck.
5. Pull out one card.
6. Lay your card facedown on your table.
7. Turn it over.
8. Gaze at that card.
9. See what leaps out at you or what feelings or insights arise.
10. Refer to this book (or another guidebook) if you're not getting a clear message—or just go ahead and trust your hunches.
11. Make your interpretation.

That's it. One question. One card. You can't mess this up!

Once you feel comfortable doing a one-card spread, you might want to move on to a two-card spread.

HOW TO DO A TWO-CARD SPREAD

Much like a one-card spread, this is pretty foolproof, too. Here's how to do it:
1. Come up with a question—ideally a question where you are comparing two options, exploring two pathways, seeking insight into two job opportunities, something like that.
2. Take a deep breath.
3. Shuffle your deck.
4. Cut the deck.
5. Pull out two cards.
6. Allow one card to represent "option A" and the other to represent "option B."
7. Lay both cards facedown on your table.
8. Turn them over.
9. Gaze at your cards.
10. What do you see? Notice what leaps out at you or what feelings or insights arise. Do you see a story unfolding in the cards? What are the differences between the two cards? Does one obviously feel like a better choice? Or do they both offer different rewards? Refer to this book (or another guidebook) if you're not getting a clear message—or just go ahead and trust your hunches.
11. Make your interpretation.

That's it. One question. Two cards. Not too complex, right? You got this. Maybe you'd like to graduate to a three-card spread!

HOW TO DO A THREE-CARD SPREAD

When you add a few more cards to your spread, you get a bit more information. Here are a couple of three-card spreads that I love:

- Past, Present, Future
- Choice One, Choice Two, Advice
- The Situation, What You Need to Know, Advice

Let's grab a few examples so you can see how these work!

Past, Present, Future

A classic! A quick look at what's happened, where you are now, and what may come.

SCENARIO Jamie has been running a successful business for three years. Recently, his business has slowed down, and he's concerned about the future. He decides to consult his Tarot deck. He asks: "What can I expect with my business if I continue on my current path?"

He pulls three cards and arranges them left to right. He begins his interpretation.

[left] PAST Knight of Wands. Jamie has put a lot of passion into his business. This passion allowed him to create a thriving business that grew quickly. Everything was moving at a brisk speed.

[center] PRESENT Six of Swords. This card shows three figures in a boat moving forward. The figures look as if they are grieving. This says that things may have been choppy, but there is movement. The current stagnancy is not permanent. He needs to continue sailing forward and perhaps explore new avenues to promote his work.

[right] FUTURE The Star. Hope and optimism return! It's very likely that this was a temporary slowdown—and not an indicator of a dying business. Things will be moving in a positive direction, and the flow should be improving shortly. The best path for Jamie is to stay on his grind and keep the faith. The future is brightening up.

Choice One, Choice Two, Advice

This is a perfect spread when you are trying to decide between two options.

SCENARIO Tenisha wants to move to a new apartment. She's considering two locations for her new home. She wants to identify the best location before she signs a contract. She pulls three cards and arranges them left to right. She begins her interpretation.

[left] CHOICE ONE The Emperor. This is a rock-solid card that indicates a sturdy foundation. It's also likely that this location is well maintained and managed—very secure. This could be a great location for her.

[center] CHOICE TWO Seven of Cups. This card indicates an illusion. Could this apartment be too good to be true? Tenisha may need to look very carefully here to see if there is something she's not seeing before diving in. For example, there may be some problems with the building that aren't being revealed. Or maybe her would-be neighbors are totally nutso. She needs to look deeper and not be swayed by initial appearances.

[right] ADVICE High Priestess. Tenisha needs to trust her gut here. Even though the first option looks better, if she is still drawn to the second place, it's worth investigating further to see what the potential issues are and whether those are things she can work with. If she gets a strong feeling to move into one place, she should trust that instinct—her gut should be the deciding factor.

The Situation, What You Need to Know, Advice

This is a spread that I created many years ago. The brilliance lies in its simplicity: a look at the situation, along with what you need to know (but may not be seeing), and advice to help you find the best path.

SCENARIO Burt is thinking about leaving his full-time job and becoming a self-employed consultant. This would allow him to spend more time with his family, and he would really enjoy the freedom of being his own boss. He asks: "I want to quit my job because I'm feeling unhappy. What do I need to know in order to make that kind of change?" He pulls three cards and arranges them left to right. He begins his interpretation.

[left] THE SITUATION Judgement. Burt is getting a "higher calling," and it's becoming harder to ignore. He's craving a more meaningful life. Because this is the card of rebirth, it's an indicator that he wants to shed his old life and start fresh. This will be a major change, but one that promises a purposeful way of life.

[center] WHAT YOU NEED TO KNOW Two of Swords. Despite that Judgement card, this one says that this plan is not clear and Burt needs to do a lot more thinking and planning before taking a big leap. It may be that his family is resistant to the idea and not sold on it yet. If they are not in alignment, he may hold back until they are on board.

[right] ADVICE Four of Swords. The best course of action at this time may be more contemplation. If Burt gives this more time, he may be able to find a path that will allow him to live his dream without jeopardizing his finances or making his family feel stressed. Because this is the card of planning, it's also a sign that becoming self-employed may require a lot more planning before it can become a reality. Burt needs to take his time and create a fully formed idea and plan before he can execute this with confidence.

One-card, two-card, and three-card spreads can keep you happily occupied for years, but they are just the beginning!

You can get mega-creative with your spreads. I recommend *Tarot Spreads: Layouts & Techniques to Empower Your Readings* by Barbara Moore for tips on how to do fancy-schmancy spreads and even invent your own for situations that are unique to your life.

Things to Keep in Mind

While practice makes perfect, here are a few good techniques can take you from rookie to reader in short order:

- Pay attention to the majorities in a spread. Are you pulling mostly Major Arcanas? If so, you may need to look at the bigger picture. Lots of aces? Fresh start ahead! A full house of kings? An important meeting. All Cups? The reading may have more to do with emotions, no matter what the question. Always remember: the majority rules.

- Are the cards mostly low numbers? If so, that may suggest the situation is at the beginning stages. Higher numbers show an end in sight.

- Draw a blank? I have three techniques for you! The first: move on to another card and come back to it later. The second: gaze at the card and see what draws your attention. Does this jog your intuition? If not, try this: describe the card. Sometimes simply describing the image begins spurring the insights.

- If you are using more than one card, pay attention to how the cards go together. What story are they telling? Are the figures interacting in any way? If so, how? Tell the story you see and notice what interpretations arise from that.

- If you get nothing, don't fret. Instead, jot down any insights you may have, put the cards away, and come back to your notes later. They may make more sense on later reflection.

- Still struggling to memorize those interpretations? Grab a marker and write prompts on your cards. Instant Tarot flash cards! (You can always buy a new deck!)

- One last tip: the cards may see potential outcomes based on the time of the reading, but nothing is ever cut in stone. If you don't like what you see, remember that you can change course. As I always say: the cards tell a story . . . but you write the ending.

- Finally, if you don't like an outcome, ask follow-up questions to see if there is a strategy or detour that might help you avoid that outcome. But keep this in mind: sometimes a negative outcome may be the red flag you need to see so that you can contemplate the direction in which you are currently heading. Don't get "mad" at your Tarot deck for revealing an unsavory or negative-looking card. Say "thank you" for the heads-up—then take corrective action to prevent that scenario from happening or continuing!

PRACTICE ROUND!

Ready to practice using your new Tarot skills?

You already know the drill: Come up with a question. Shuffle your deck. Cut the deck. Choose a spread. Rock it out. (Then repeat!)

Recording your readings in a journal can be a great way to improve your skills because you can study and refer to your readings later. From time to time, review your past readings to see how events unfolded. What worked out? What didn't? What new insights did you discover? Here's a good format to use to record you readings:

Date:
My question:
Spread that I chose to do:
Cards that showed up:
My insights, feelings, and interpretation:

KEEP PRACTICING

Falling in love with Tarot? I love seeing people get passionate about Tarot, and, in my opinion, the world could use more skilled, insightful readers. The more the merrier. But it takes time to master the art of Tarot.

Which means you need to be patient and keep practicing. Like any skill, the more time you put in, the better you'll get. Personally, I did Tarot for about ten years (starting at age fifteen) totally for free, just for my own pleasure and education, before I ever started charging money to do a reading.

If you're doing readings for yourself and your friends, that's a great start. (That's how I started, too!) Keep going! Try to get superfamiliar with your deck and do readings for lots of different types of people—men, women, different ages, different backgrounds, and all types of different questions and needs—to gain experience. Do readings for yourself. This is the best way to practice, because no one knows you better than you do.

But most important, have fun!

RESOURCES

Here are a few of my all-time favorite Tarot decks—aside from the classic Rider Waite deck, of course:

Baroque Bohemian Cats' Tarot, Magic Realist Press (September 1, 2004)

The Fountain Tarot, The Fountain Tarot (April/May, 2015)

Gaian Tarot by Joanna Powell Colbert, Schiffer (June 28, 2016)

Hanson-Roberts Tarot by Hanson-Roberts, US Games Systems, Inc. (October 1, 1995)

Morgan-Greer Tarot by Bill F. Greer, US Games Systems Inc.; Cards edition (July 25, 2011)

Robin Wood Tarot by Robin Wood, Llewellyn Publications; Cards edition (September 8, 2002)

Here are some Tarot books that I love:

The Complete Book of Tarot Reversals by Mary K. Greer, Llewellyn Publications (March 8, 2002)

Holistic Tarot: An Integrative Approach to Using Tarot for Personal Growth by Benebell Wen, North Atlantic Books (January 6, 2015)

Learning the Tarot: A Tarot Book for Beginners by Joan Bunning, Weiser Books (October 1, 1998)

The Pictorial Key to the Tarot by A. E. Waite, Dover Publications (June 10, 2005)

The Secret Language of Tarot by Wald Amberstone and Ruth Ann Amberstone, Weiser Books (April 1, 2008)

Seventy-Eight Degrees of Wisdom: A Book of Tarot by Rachel Pollack, Weiser Books (September 1, 2007)

Tarot Spreads: Layouts & Techniques to Empower Your Readings by Barbara Moore, Llewellyn Publications (April 8, 2012)

21 Ways to Read a Tarot Card by Mary K. Greer, Llewellyn Publications (May 8, 2006)

Understanding the Tarot Court by Mary K. Greer and Tom Little, Llewellyn Publications; first edition (April 8, 2004)

Here are some great Tarot blogs and other online resources:

Aeclectic Tarot, aeclectic.net/tarot/: A fabulous resource for Tarot deck and book reviews.

Benebell Wen, benebellwen.com: Smart, taut writing and solid deck reviews.

Beth Owl's Daughter, owlsdaughter.com: Wise insights on Tarot from a Tarot master.

Learning the Tarot, learntarot.com: Joan Bunning's wonderful site and the best online resource for budding Tarot readers.

Little Fox Tarot, littlefoxtarot.com: Some of the best Tarot writing on the web.

Little Red Tarot, littleredtarot.com: This Tarot blog is a favorite destination for Tarot lovers.

Louise Androlia, louiseandrolia.com: Excellent Tarot writing and tutorials.

Mary Greer's Blog, marygreer.wordpress.com: The grande dame of Tarot!

The Numinous, the-numinous.com: Thoroughly modern and stylish Tarot blogging.

Paige Z's Tarot and Tea, paigezaferiou.com: A whimsical, modern view on Tarot and magic.

Tarot by Hilary, tarotbyhilary.com: Smart Tarot thoughts for readers of all levels.

Tarot Elements, tarotelements.com: One of the best Tarot blogs out there.

The Tarot Garden, tarotgarden.com: A great selection of hard-to-find Tarot decks.

The Tarot School, tarotschool.com: A great learning resource for all Tarot levels.

Tarot Thrones, tarot-thrones.com: This is a clever blog focused on the Court Cards.

US Games, usgamesinc.com: The printer of the Rider Waite Tarot and other wonderful decks.

Traveling? Here are a handful of my favorite metaphysical shops around the United States:

New York: Enchantments, enchantmentsincnyc.com
Milwaukee: Free Spirit Crystals, freespiritcrystals.com
Minneapolis: Eye of Horus, eyeofhorus.biz
Portland: New Renaissance Bookshop,
    newrenbooks.com

Love this coloring book? Here is another instructional coloring book that you might enjoy published by the great folks at Sounds True:

The Shakti Coloring Book: Goddesses, Mandalas, and the Power of Sacred Geometry by Ekabhumi Charles Ellik, Sounds True (July 1, 2015)

ACKNOWLEDGMENTS

Creating this coloring book was a labor of love—big, passionate love—and also coffee, chocolate, tiny hippo-shaped cookies filled with more chocolate, crystals, and . . . a glass or two of wine.

This book would not have happened without support from the following peeps:

The wonderful staff at Sounds True. Thank you. Words cannot express my gratitude.

Jennifer Brown, acquisitions editor of Sound True, for approaching me with this idea.

Gretel Gene Hakanson, my fabulous editor, for polishing this book to perfection.

Leslie Brown, my production editor, for all your patience and guidance.

Alexandra Franzen, my dear friend and most trusted right-hand woman. You always help me find the right words at the right time.

Megan Lang, my favorite word nerd. Your eagle eyes catch what mine don't.

Mary K. Greer for all your support over the years and with this book.

My friends Andy Matzner, Brianna Saussy, Rachel Pollack, Joanna Powell Colbert, Donnaleigh de le Rose, Georgianna Boehnke, Suzi Dronzek, Hilary Parry, Barbara Moore and Lisa Novak, Jennifer Louden, Ruth Ann and Wald Amberstone, Fabeku Fatunmise, Chris Zydel, Guy and Jackie Dayen, Damien Echols and Lorri Davis, Angelo Nasios, Jessica Schumacher, Andrew McGregor, and countless others (there is not enough room to name you all, but you know who you are). You inspire me!

My amazing yoga students and Tarot clients. It's been my honor to serve you all these years.

My children, Megan and Nick. You've made me one proud momma!

And most of all, my husband, Terry. You've always believed in me and with your support, everything is possible.

I am eternally grateful. We did it, team!

ABOUT THE AUTHOR

Hey! It's me, Theresa Reed.

As a Catholic schoolgirl with a superstitious mother and a grandma who felt omens like other folks feel arthritis, it's not too surprising that Tarot, astrology, and other intuitive arts would become my driving fascination—and my life's work.

I picked up my first Tarot deck at age fifteen and kick-started my career by performing readings on my little sister. (Most of her questions were about the cute boys in class. Some things never change.)

Thirtyish years later, I've done readings on thousands of clients—from teachers to recovering addicts to new mothers to angst-ridden teens to small-business owners and powerhouse CEOs.

In addition to doing private, confidential Tarot readings, I also lead Tarot workshops, speak at Tarot conferences, cohost a podcast for spiritual business owners, and dip my toes into lots of other Tarot-licious projects.

(On top of running my Tarot biz, I also run a side business teaching yoga to people who feel like "misfits" at other yoga studios. Quirky, wobbly, and not so bendy? You're my kind of yogi!)

When people ask me, "Why Tarot, Theresa?" I've got a pretty straightforward answer:

I love helping people make better decisions and lead happier lives, and Tarot is the best tool I've found to do just that.

Should you choose to hire me for a reading, I promise to deliver my clearest intuitive hits, my lifetime of experience, my tough-lovin' wisdom, and mad respect for you and your journey.

You can find me online at thetarotlady.com. I also hang out on Facebook, Twitter, and Instagram, and you'll find all my social media coordinates on my site.

Thank you for reading and coloring your way through this book. I hope your Tarot deck becomes one of your new favorite decision-making tools, and I am wishing you all the success in the world.

Many blessings!

ABOUT SOUNDS TRUE

Sounds True is a multimedia publisher whose mission is to inspire and support personal transformation and spiritual awakening. Founded in 1985 and located in Boulder, Colorado, we work with many of the leading spiritual teachers, thinkers, healers, and visionary artists of our time. We strive with every title to preserve the essential "living wisdom" of the author or artist. It is our goal to create products that not only provide information to a reader or listener, but that also embody the quality of a wisdom transmission.

For those seeking genuine transformation, Sounds True is your trusted partner. At SoundsTrue.com you will find a wealth of free resources to support your journey, including exclusive weekly audio interviews, free downloads, interactive learning tools, and other special savings on all our titles.

To learn more, please visit SoundsTrue.com/freegifts or call us toll-free at 800.333.9185.